DAOIST NEI GONG

DAOIST NEI GONG

The Philosophical Art of Change

DAMO MITCHELL

FOREWORD BY DR CINDY ENGEL

SINGING
DRAGON

LONDON AND PHILADELPHIA

First published in 2011
by Singing Dragon
an imprint of Jessica Kingsley Publishers
73 Collier Street
London N1 9BE, UK
and
400 Market Street, Suite 400
Philadelphia, PA 19106, USA

www.singingdragon.com

Library of Congress Cataloging in Publication Data
A CIP catalog record for this book is available from the Library of Congress

British Library Cataloguing in Publication Data
A CIP catalogue record for this book is available from the British Library

ISBN 978 1 84819 065 8
eISBN 978 0 85701 033 9

Printed and bound in the United States

I dedicate this book to all sincere practitioners of the internal arts.
May the search for truth be fruitful and rewarding.

DISCLAIMER

The author and publisher of this material are not responsible in any way whatsoever for any injury that may occur through reading or practising the exercises outlined in this book.

The exercises and practices may be too strenuous or risky for some people and so you should consult a qualified doctor before attempting anything from this book. It is also advised that you proceed under the guidance of an experienced teacher of the internal arts to avoid injury and confusion.

Note that any form of internal exercise is not a replacement for conventional health practices, medicines or any form of psychotherapy.

CONTENTS

List of Figures, Tables and Boxes

FIGURES

TABLES

BOXES

FOREWORD

Throughout history numerous cultures have developed processes of human transformation using only aspects of mind. Practitioners are able to transform their nature – their physical, mental, emotional and spiritual selves – using attention and intention. All of these transformative techniques demand one thing – practice. The amount of practice that is needed requires a certain type of person – a dedicated, dare I say, obsessive person, who will put all of their attention and intention in the desired direction.

This level of focus is extremely difficult in a modern multimedia, information-overloaded life style. It takes perseverance and determination to make progress. This work is not just an interest for Damo. It is his life.

As a fellow Qi Gong student, I underestimated Damo's abilities, put them down to youthful confidence; but as soon as I saw him move and felt the effect of his intention on my energetic system, it was obvious he was working on a very different level to anyone else I had so far encountered. He was doing more than just learning about the internal arts. He was exploring, experiencing, expanding and developing the teachings he received for hours a day, everyday. Whereas I was being taught the same thing over and over and still not getting it, he only needed the slightest exposure to information in order to understand it.

Over the years, I have watched him expand and develop the wealth of traditional knowledge into a system that can be expressed in a modern world. This long-awaited book is the first to share these explorations without the cloak of secrecy normally surrounding the topic.

Dr Cindy Engel
Author of Wild Health

PREFACE

Since my early childhood I have been studying the Eastern arts in one form or another. I was fortunate enough to be born into a family of martial artists and seekers of the way. I was exposed to the arts of combat, medicine and spirituality early enough that their logic and practices began to seep into the deeper layers of my psyche.

This practice blossomed into a passion which often borders on an obsession. Throughout my early and mid teens I studied the martial systems and sought to obtain raw physical power. By my late teens and twenties my interest had been taken over by the path of the internal systems. In particular the link between practices such as Qi Gong and meditation caught my interest and I realised how all of my martial studies had only been laying the foundation for this aspect of the Daoist arts. The result of these studies, which have taken me across Europe and Asia, is the system which I teach within my own school which is based in the United Kingdom. The foundation of this system is Nei Gong.

Nei Gong is the attainment of real internal skill through the practice of the internal arts. It is the awakening of the energy body and cultivation of our consciousness. It is the philosophical art of change which permeates all Daoist practices.

In this book I present the principle and practices of Daoist internal arts. I outline various exercises which may be used as tools to understand Nei Gong. It is my hope that readers will explore the guidelines and practices from this book and see how it fits in with their own practices. Perhaps practitioners will take some aspects of the training only or recognise elements of the training which they are already studying. This is fine. Nei Gong is not a system of exercises.

It is a series of internal changes which a person may go through in order to follow a path to Dao. The way onto the Nei Gong path is through practices like Taiji or Qi Gong. I hope that by the end of the book readers will be able to understand how Taiji and Qi Gong are only tools to bring about change; understanding this is the key to understanding Nei Gong.

There are many teachers today who seek to adapt exercises to suit modern people. Qi Gong and Taiji were changed to suit the masses and systems were developed which could be learnt in a much shorter time than their traditional counterparts. This is a positive development which has enabled the internal arts to flourish and countless people, who would otherwise have found these arts inaccessible, to experience the benefits they may bring. However, there are many people out there who are frustrated with this situation. They have read accounts of the skills of the past masters and join internal arts classes in order to pursue this path. They are soon disappointed when they find that traditional skills like this require traditional teaching which is increasingly scarce, either here in the West or in Asia. When putting this book together I have not shied away from discussing the lengths of time required for understanding each stage of Nei Gong nor the inherent risks attached to this kind of training. Whilst practitioners may take some of the health benefits from Nei Gong with only a moderate amount of practice, true skill can only come to those who train diligently over a long period of time.

Some aspects of Nei Gong training are controversial, in particular some of the skills which can be drawn from these practices. Many practitioners do not believe such skills exist. The Chinese compare this state of mind to being like a frog in a well. The frog cannot see the outside world and so believes his tiny environment to be all that exists. Like the frog in the well, many practitioners limit their own growth and development through training with a closed mind. This is not the way to Dao.

Throughout the book I have dotted poignant lines from the *Dao De Jing*. I did not feel that any attempt to outline traditional Daoist practices would be complete without some words from the 'original Daoist' himself.

I myself am a perpetual student of the Dao. I continue to study and develop as well as teach. I hope that this book will serve to help others on their path or act as a catalyst for their own personal exploration of the Daoist arts.

ACKNOWLEDGEMENTS

First, I would like to express my gratitude to the many teachers and guides I have had over the years; without their guidance I would not be the person I am today. Thank you to my friends and parents, Paul and Chris, for starting me on my journey into the martial arts at the age of four.

Thank you to the various people who helped me in the writing and production of this book. Thanks to my good friend Dr Cindy Engel who has provided encouragement and support through the whole project as well as kindly writing the Foreword for this book.

Much gratitude to Daniel Reid whose writing has always been an inspiration and whose words of endorsement mean a great deal to me.

Thank you to my good friend Spencer Hill who has been involved in this project from its outset and who helped me turn my thoughts into writing in the first place.

Thank you to Joe Andrews for his excellent line drawings, and to Lydia Beaumont who kindly posed for the photos on page 129.

Thank you to Steve 'Zom' Galloway who helped with proofreading and suggestions on how the text could be made more accessible.

Thank you to the good people of Singing Dragon publishers and especially Jessica Kingsley for having faith in the book and for bringing my teachings to print.

Last but not least, thank you to my partner and best friend, Roni, for her support and putting up with the piles of paper dotted around our study.

NOTES ON ROMANISATION OF PINYIN

Throughout this book I have used the Pinyin system of Romanisation for the majority of Chinese words. Please note that much of the theory in this book differs greatly from Western science. The Chinese approach to understanding the organs of the body, for example, is based around the function of their energetic system rather than their physical anatomy. To distinguish the two different uses of organ descriptions I have capitalised the terms when they are meant from a Chinese point of view. For example: 'Heart' means the energetic system whilst 'heart' means the physical organ from a Western point of view.

Nei Gong theory differs a little from Chinese medicine theory with which an acupuncturist would be familiar. These differences are largely due to different aspects of the energetic system being emphasised in the training.

Many of these teachings come from the original guidelines outlined by Laozi and his contemporaries. Where relevant I have included short sections from the *Dao De Jing*, the classical text of Laozi. These sections are from my own translation from the classical Chinese and so any errors in translation are my fault entirely. Any lines from the *Dao De Jing* are indicated in italics.

CHAPTER 1

INTRODUCTION TO NEI GONG

When President Nixon travelled to China in 1972 (Buell and Ramey 2004) he witnessed Traditional Chinese Medicine being practised within hospitals and saw how, through the use of acupuncture needles, surgeons were able to carry out operations on fully conscious patients without them feeling pain. Since this time, various Chinese internal arts have been spreading to and becoming popular within the West.

One of these arts is Qi Gong (Chi Kung) or 'Energy Skill'. Qi Gong is practised by tens of thousands of people every day in parks, their homes or even as part of a recommended daily routine prescribed by Western medical practitioners. Through a combination of controlled breathing, slow gentle movements and a calm mind, practitioners of Qi Gong enable their internal energy (Qi) to flow more efficiently through the various internal pathways of the human energy system. This leads to increased health, a stronger immune system and lower stress levels, amongst other benefits.

In the West, Qi Gong or the associated art of Taiji and the benefits of these two practices can be felt by anyone willing to look for a local class. What is far less known is another Chinese practice: that of Nei Gong.

In China there are three main spiritual traditions: Confucianism, Buddhism and Daoism. These three great philosophies have dictated

Chinese culture and their arts for centuries. For the most part these three traditions have managed to live and flourish alongside each other and this has resulted in a pooling of methods and philosophies. It is for this reason that it is impossible to say that any of the Chinese arts is born from any one of the three. Qi Gong, Taiji and Nei Gong are no exception; although primarily Daoist in nature, they also have elements of Confucianism and Buddhism contained within them.

WHAT IS NEI GONG?

Nei Gong can be translated as 'Internal Skill'. Defined simply it is: 'The process by which a person may condition their physical body, cultivate their internal universe and elevate their consciousness.'

Nei Gong has long been considered the most advanced and most complete of the internal practices of China. It was kept a closely guarded secret long after Qi Gong and Taiji were leaked to the public of China and the West. Only in recent times have people begun to be aware of the term Nei Gong and there is still a great deal of confusion as to what it means within the internal arts community.

Nei Gong is not a specific set of exercises or movements. Rather it is a series of stages that a person may move through in their practice given the correct instruction. In many ways it is similar to the more advanced processes inherent within Indian Yoga once a practitioner has moved past the basic training of Asanas. The Qi Gong exercises which are being practised every day by so many people serve as the tools for working through this process. Practising the movements of Qi Gong on their own will give you good health and mental clarity but they will not take you any further than this unless you understand the principles of Nei Gong and how to implement them into your training. This book will outline the principles of Nei Gong and give practitioners of Qi Gong, Taiji and other internal arts a better idea of how these arts fit together and where they can lead.

Nei Gong first serves to condition the physical body and then the energy system. These two stages serve to provide the foundation for the third step which is direct work with the very elements which make up our consciousness. It is important that we keep in mind the three stages of development shown in Figure 1.1.

Figure 1.1 Three Stages of Nei Gong Training

Each of the three stages in our training requires that we work with and increase our body's ability to produce three substances which we know as Jing, Qi and Shen within Daoism. They are linked to the three stages of development as shown in Figure 1.2.

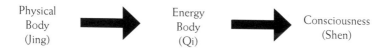

Figure 1.2 Three Nei Gong Substances of Daoism

During the practice of Nei Gong you will go through various changes and stages in your development. The first change you will begin to notice is an improvement in your overall health and well-being. From here you will begin to notice differences in your personality and outlook on life. The higher stages of training begin to alter the way your mind works and perceives existence. It is at this stage that the Daoist meditative practices of internal alchemy become entwined within Nei Gong.

What follows is a brief list of the changes that are most likely to take place within you during the course of your Nei Gong practice. This list was drawn from my own personal experiences as well as from observation of my students over the years.

- First, your muscles begin to relax and soften. Old tensions begin to release and the mobility of your joints increases dramatically. After several months practice it begins to feel as though you have limbs which are made of jelly.

- Old injuries begin to vanish. In my case it was injuries sustained during my martial arts practice which began to slowly fade away. It is surprising to see exactly how much discomfort you have been living with. I often find within my classes that people have unconsciously been living with great amounts of pain and they only realise when their old injuries begin to fade.

- Your immune system begins to improve dramatically and some long-term illnesses begin to vanish. The Nei Gong training at this stage has empowered your body to begin working more efficiently. It begins to seek out and get rid of pathogens and toxins which most people have stored for many years.

- Your mind begins to calm down and for the first time many people experience what it means to have true stillness for short periods of time within the centre of their minds. Stress is not really something we experience during the course of our lives; it is only a product of how we react to outside stimuli. The Nei Gong training has begun to change how we react to outside factors and so we begin to experience life without becoming stressed by it.

- Now your bodily alignments begin to change as deeply rooted tensions fade. Many people experience clicks and cracks during their practice as their bones begin to shift into a more natural and correct position. Much like receiving a Chiropractic session, people begin to lose even more tension around the joints. As this tension begins to vanish, people literally gain an extra inch or so in height as their bones free up and their joints open. This has the advantage of increasing the efficiency of your body and your physical strength. It always gives me joy as a teacher to see how people's postures improve and the look of relief upon their faces as they begin to straighten up.

- The energy system begins to awaken and people begin to experience the more 'unusual' side of Nei Gong training. It is at this point in their study that people begin to experience the movement of their internal energy and how it is linked to their emotions. There are various 'releases' at this stage and people find that they become emotionally more stable in their daily lives.

- Later the body begins to operate on a purely energetic level and people find that they feel very light. They feel loose and comfortable when they move and every aspect of their life begins to become fluid and natural. Daoists say that at this point they are returning to Ziran (Nature).

• The basic levels of Nei Gong training are now complete and the practitioner can begin to work directly with their Shen. These stages are explained later in the book. For now it is enough to know some of the benefits which take place during the early stages of practice.

WHY PRACTISE NEI GONG?

It is always difficult to answer this question when asked. At first I was adamant that all people should practise Nei Gong and much like a 'door to door philosophy peddler' I would try to convince anybody who would engage me in conversation. In many instances these people would attend one of my classes or courses but in the vast majority of cases they would find the training too arduous and so leave after only a few sessions. Although they recognised the benefits of the training they did not deem these benefits worth the time and effort required.

I have since come to realise that people simply move in to Nei Gong training when the time is right for them. It is more of a calling than anything else. It just seems that some people are ready to begin bringing about positive changes within the various layers of their being. Many of my students get frustrated at this; they are deeply passionate about their training and desperately want their friends and family to understand. I know that their conviction is born out of compassion, they simply want others to experience the healthy and happy benefits that they have drawn from their practice, but they begin to realise after some time that what I have said is true. People do not move into Nei Gong training through advertising or convincing, they simply come when the time is right for them. I apologise to any readers who are hoping for a better reason to practice Nei Gong but I cannot give one. If you are not drawn to the practice then the time is simply not right for you.

For those who have begun the training, they have the pleasure of experiencing the Daoist ideals of health, longevity and clarity of mind. These are truly treasures which enable us to enjoy and get the most out of the rest of our lives. These three alone are reason enough for me.

Box 1.1 Who Should Not Train

Whilst the internal arts can bring great benefits to those who practise them it is important to recognise that they are not suitable for everybody. There are some groups of people for whom Nei Gong in particular poses sometimes severe risks.

Children and teenagers should not study Nei Gong. Qi Gong on its own is fine provided that it is not used to move through the various internal processes of Nei Gong. There should be no direct work with the Dan Tien or any aspect of the energy system. Young people who wish to study Qi Gong should focus on relaxing and conditioning the body as well as stretching and learning to breathe effectively. Usually in China it is considered better for younger people to study the external martial arts which will prepare them physically for more advanced internal training in the future.

The reason for this is fairly simple. Young people and teenagers are subject to a greater amount of emotional disturbances. The teenage years in particular are full of emotional upsets, anguish and frustration for the majority of young people. The emotional aspect of the Heart-Mind has not yet fully formed and it is not until our early twenties that we begin to settle down a little emotionally. The emotional state we settle into may not be a very healthy one in many cases but at least it should be considerably more stable with fewer 'swings' from high to low. Much Nei Gong work has a direct influence on the emotions and our consciousness. We should not do anything to interfere with the emotions on this level until we have reached a sufficiently stable age.

Pregnant women should steer clear of the internal arts. Whilst the risks are low, they are still risks. The internal work can have various effects on an unborn child. An art such as Yoga is far more suitable during pregnancy.

Those with a history of mental illness should be careful when beginning Nei Gong and seek guidance from an experienced teacher throughout. Any form of work with the mind can be damaging to those with a mental illness if it is not carried out correctly.

You should also not train when sick or when in an emotionally heightened state. Wait until your illness is passed or you have reached a more stable emotional state prior to beginning practice.

THE STAGES OF PRACTICE

Traditionally there was no sequential order for moving through the various principles of Nei Gong. This may have been suitable for Chinese students but in the West we have a different way of thinking. Society has dictated that we are 'goal orientated' and this means we need a process to work through. The order I have put together here is the structure I use to teach my own students. Over the last few years of implementing Nei Gong in my classes I have found this to be the most effective way of teaching these complex principles to everybody. I will explain the various stages briefly below.

1. Conditioning and Preparing the Physical Body

2. Regulation of the Breath and the Mind

3. Beginning the Conversion of Jing to Qi

4. Awakening the Energy System

5. Movement of the Yang Qi

6. Attainment of Internal Vibration

7. Conversion of Qi to Shen

8. Conversion of Shen to Dao

Conditioning and Preparing the Physical Body
A proper foundation must be built within the physical realm of your body. Here we must work on our alignments, relaxation, softness, flexibility and the opening and closing of our joints.

We must not neglect this stage if we wish to progress steadily in our training. We must also return to this stage time and time again to ensure that our body remains healthy and is working efficiently. Quite simply, our body is our workshop for Nei Gong practice. If we do not look after our workspace then we will not produce good results.

Regulation of the Breath and the Mind
We will see later how our breathing and mindset are integral parts of our training. They serve as the 'intermediaries' between our physical body, our energy body and our consciousness. It is important that we spend time early on in our training working on the condition of our breathing and mindset.

Beginning the Conversion of Jing to Qi

This is the first stage in our training where we begin to work with the various energetic substances of the body. We are beginning to learn about and refine the internal vibrations which move through us during our practice. This is the point where we are able to begin drawing a strong link between our physical and energetic bodies. If we are not able to make these two systems work efficiently as one unit then our efforts will amount to little.

Awakening the Energy System

This stage of training is not as complex as many teachers make it out to be. Once we strip away the flowery language and all of the useless adornments it is possible to see the root of all of the internal arts. A lot of practitioners never manage to achieve this stage of development for the simple reason that they have not developed a strong foundation in the previous stages. Much of the Daoist teachings concern this stage but practitioners should be patient in preparing their body and mind for this point in the Nei Gong process.

Movement of the Yang Qi

Once we have awakened the energy body we are able to begin moving the Yang Qi through our system. This is the time of rejuvenation for which Daoism is most well known. The quality of our internal energy is improved and allowed to move freely within us which in turn nourishes and nurtures the body's tissues. A practitioner who has reached this stage of Nei Gong training is easy to spot as their body takes on an unnaturally fluid quality that at the same time belies a great core strength.

Attainment of Internal Vibration

At this stage we begin to understand the various substances and functions of the body as vibrational frequencies. We have linked our mind to our internal energy and we are able to direct our movements with a simple thought. This is a profound step which leads us to be able to understand the nature of our relationship to the outer universe.

Conversion of Qi to Shen

We are now ready to begin working on altering the nature of our internal energy so that it nourishes our consciousness. At this stage we begin to tap into mind-altering levels of comprehension which followers of all spiritual traditions have strived to reach. This is a high stage of practice which is accompanied by clear signs of progress.

Conversion of Shen to Dao

The final stage of Nei Gong is the conversion of pure consciousness to emptiness. I am afraid that my understanding ends here as I am working on this stage myself. It is almost certain that your Nei Gong can be taken further but I only like to talk about things that I have experienced. I only have theoretical teachings on further practice of Nei Gong but since I have not reached them I cannot write about them with confidence. Too many times people pass on information which is based on theoretical understanding rather than direct experience; this is how untruths and misinformation are passed on.

PHILOSOPHY IS THE ROOT OF NEI GONG

The East is rightly famous as the source of many great philosophies. In order for an internal art to be a valid product of the East it has to adhere to various philosophical roots. It is common for contemporary teachers of the internal arts in both the East and the West to ignore philosophy and focus entirely on the practices which they have been taught. This approach will severely limit the levels of attainment to be had from your practice. Philosophy is the root of all internal arts and Nei Gong is no exception.

'How do I understand the origin?

Return to the beginning of course!'

The core truth of Nei Gong is that after we are born we begin to grow sick. As soon as we interact with the outside world we are already moving along the timeline to destruction which the Daoists simply called our 'Ming'. If we are to attain good health and spiritual liberation then we have to learn how to reverse this process – known as 'returning to the source'. This travel back to an original state may seem slightly paradoxical to Western minds, but to the ancient Chinese it was a logical progression. They also believed that the changes which take place within us as we age are a reflection of the processes taking place within the universe around us, and for this reason they used metaphorical language taken from our external environment to explain what was happening inside us. This was known as the link between the macrocosm and the microcosm.

In Daoist thought the outer environment which surrounds us is the macrocosm. The inside of our bodies is the microcosm. The microcosm relies on the macrocosm for existence and vice versa. The various energetic shifts which take place within the macrocosm are reflected within the microcosm and in this way our 'inner universe' is a direct replication of the 'outer universe' (see Figure 1.3).

It is important to understand that the microcosm and the macrocosm are only such when compared to each other. Contained within the microcosm are further microcosms or 'inner universes' contained within 'inner universes'. To our molecules and atoms our physical body is actually the macrocosm. If we can understand this principle then we have built a strong foundation for our study of the nature of the Dao.

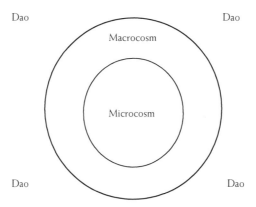

Figure 1.3 The Microcosm and the Macrocosm

Our relationship to the outer environment can be further understood by looking at the principle of the 'three powers' within Daoist cosmology. The three powers are the energies of Heaven, Man and Earth.

Heaven is the manifestation of pure unadulterated Yang energy whilst Earth is the physical manifestation of Yin energy. The energy of human beings is a combination of these two entities and we are totally dependent upon Heaven and Earth for our existence. A major concern of the Daoist arts is reconnecting to these

Figure 1.4 The Three Powers

two energies so that we may utilise them for our own ends. This is a completely natural part of our energetic awakening and an important part of the Nei Gong process. I have had students who were scared by the concept of connecting themselves to the energy of Heaven and Earth but they have forgotten one of the most important factors when approaching the study of something complex like Nei Gong: you must cut through the flowery language and try to experience exactly what it means. Remember that we are trying to look at the root of the tree and not get distracted by all of its branches and leaves.

As human beings it is often the case that we have forgotten that we are part of the wider cosmos that the Daoists named Heaven and Earth. As time goes on we move further and further away from our natural state of being and lose touch with the subtle forces of the planet. How can we as creatures develop spiritually if we have completely forgotten our root? We strive to increase our intellect through science and physical means but all we do is move further from the truth that lies at the core of our being. We seek happiness through material wealth rather than satisfaction with our connection to the cosmos. This is one of the key factors within both Daoist philosophy and practice.

DAO AND THE WUJI

The Dao is the original creative power of the universe: the primordial chaos from which all existence sprang forth. It is both 'formless' and 'infinite'; according to the teachings of Laozi its only manifestation within the realm of man is through our consciousness. The Dao contains the inexhaustible potential for all of life and if we are able to attach our minds to the energy of the Dao we are able to understand the very nature of existence. This is obviously a very complex concept to grasp and in order to do so we must 'experience' the Dao rather than simply learn about it theoretically.

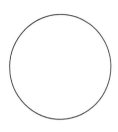

Figure 1.5 Wuji

'The Dao that can be walked

Is not the eternal path.

That which can be named

Is not the eternal Dao.'

The vast non-entity of the Dao existed before anything else. It is a combination of the two poles of opposition known simply as Yin and Yang. Prior to creation, Yin and Yang were not differentiated; they were merged into a swirling mass of kinetic power which is usually drawn within Daoist cosmology as a simple unbroken circle (see Figure 1.5).

Another name for this energy is Wuji, which simply means 'without extremities'. Wuji is the manner in which the Dao manifests within the spiritual realm of existence. It is an unending mass of information and power which forms the seed for both the energetic and physical realms. The nature of the power known as Wuji is utter stillness and the information contained within Wuji lays dormant. In Western theory Wuji could be compared to the point prior to the 'Big Bang' taking place.

Within the seat of human consciousness lies this stillness containing dormant information. The state of Wuji sits at the very core of our being and contains the 'blue prints' for every aspect of our physical, mental and spiritual selves. We call these 'blue prints' our congenital nature. When we are born, our congenital nature shines forth but as we begin to age and interact with other people our consciousness becomes distorted and the congenital nature becomes buried deep within us.

The resulting state of being is known as 'acquired' within Daoism, it is this acquired nature that we need to free ourselves from. Only then can we retrieve our original state of being and thus reconnect with Wuji and the Dao.

THE MOTIVE FORCE OF CREATION: TAIJI

It is an important Daoist concept that stillness cannot exist without movement. When an extreme state of tranquillity and calm is reached there will be born forth a spontaneous and natural form of movement which the Daoists named Taiji.

Taiji was born forth from the centre of Wuji. It manifested as a spiralling energetic wave as shown in Figure 1.6.

This spiralling wave moved outwards from the centre of Wuji and began to divide the spiritual power of Wuji into two extremes known as Yin and Yang.

One way to try and understand the nature of Wuji and Taiji is by looking at the two elements in the following way:

Figure 1.6 The Spiral Force: Taiji

Wuji contains the potential for existence but it is simply a blank canvas. Only when the movement of Taiji comes into play is existence projected onto the blank canvas of Wuji. Herein lies the one of the most confusing elements of Daoism and yet at the same time it is the key to unlocking the nature of our true selves: if Taiji serves to provide only a projection of existence, is it real? The Daoist concept is that distortions take place only because of the poles of Yin and Yang. Taiji projects a reality according to Yin and Yang onto Wuji and so is it the real world or is it fake? This is a question which comes up time and time again throughout your Nei Gong and, later, meditation practice. The answer can only be understood experientially, not intellectually.

Whenever there is any energetic shift within the universe it is due to the power of Taiji which acts as a catalyst for the processes of change, development and progress. It is for this reason that we know Taiji as the 'motive force of creation'.

In Daoist philosophy there can be no stillness without movement and vice versa. If a state of complete tranquillity and stillness is achieved then a spontaneous and natural movement will come into being. This is the force of Taiji.

YIN AND YANG

Through the spiralling power of Taiji, Yin and Yang were created. These two extremes were originally two parts that combined to form the great Dao.

Yin and Yang are well known in Traditional Chinese Medicine as well as Eastern philosophy and even people who have never had any contact with Eastern thought are likely to have heard of Yin and Yang although they will often have an incorrect understanding of them.

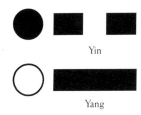

Yin

Yang

Figure 1.7 Yin and Yang

Figure 1.8 The Taiji Symbol

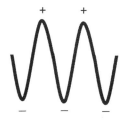

Figure 1.9 Vibrational Frequency

Yin is often referred to as being dark and feminine whilst Yang is referred to as being bright and masculine. A better way to understand Yin and Yang is through the extremes of stillness and movement.

Yin is normally represented by the colour black or in Yi Jing theory a broken line. Yang is the colour white or a solid line. see Figure 1.7.

If we again look at Wuji as our blank canvas then Yin and Yang are the elements which are projected onto it. At this point though, there are only extremes, nothing in between. Life is obviously not made purely of extremes. There is not just dark and light, there is every possible gradient which can exist between these poles. Everything between absolute light and absolute dark is made up of a combination of the two. There are never any constants between light and dark, only a perpetual shifting between the two extremes. The force that brings about the shift between the two poles is Taiji. When the spiralling energy of Taiji is added to the extremes of Yin and Yang we get the symbol in Figure 1.8.

The interchange between Yin and Yang is manifested within nature as a vibrational frequency as shown in Figure 1.9. Positive (+) is Yang and negative (-) is Yin; these are the peaks and troughs that form the vibration.

Everything in the universe, tangible and intangible, is created from various vibrational frequencies. Zoom in close enough with a microscope and every atom in its smallest part is made up of a vibration. If you look at existence in this way it is possible to see how Yin, Yang and Taiji combine to create everything in the universe from emptiness.

The various vibrational frequencies of energy that can exist within the energetic realm are represented by the eight sacred symbols known as trigrams or Gua. These eight symbols are outlined in the *Yi Jing* (*I Ching*) or *Classic of Change*. This sacred text contains a mathematical philosophy which explains the various energetic fluctuations within the universe.

The eight Gua are made up of a combination of broken and solid lines. A broken line represents Yin and a solid line represents Yang. It is not necessary to fully understand the Yi Jing in order to practise Nei Gong. It is enough to understand that they are a combination of Yin and Yang elements and that each one shows a different vibrational frequency.

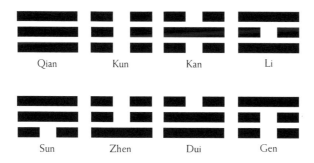

Figure 1.10 The Eight Sacred Symbols, Gua

An even distribution of Yin and Yang creates one of two Gua. These are Kan and Li or 'Water' and 'Fire'. Every other Gua has an uneven distribution of Yin and Yang although this cannot really be understood until the vibrational frequency of a Gua is looped over and over into a long wave such as shown in Figure 1.11 with the Kan Gua.

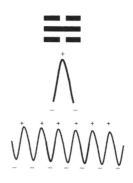

The Kan Gua (Water) has an even distribution of Yin and Yang when it is combined into a constant vibration. Li (Fire) will produce an almost identical wave with the only difference being the originating energy. An origin of Yin will produce Kan whilst an origin of Yang will produce Li. Figure 1.11 shows an origin point of Yin so it is known as Kan.

Figure 1.11 The Kan Gua, Kan Gua as a Wave, Kan Gua Vibration (from top to bottom)

31

The frequencies of Kan and Li are the prime representations of Yin and Yang evenly mixing and so are shown in the following symbol (Figure 1.12) for Yin and Yang, which predates the Taiji symbol. This circular symbol is made up of concentric rings and shows the manifestation of the two energies which are constructed from an equal proportion of movement and stillness. The central white circle represents emptiness and shows that at the heart of movement lies the potential for perfect stillness or Wuji (Figure 1.12).

Figure 1.12 Li and Kan Constructing Yang and Yin

THE WU XING

The next stage in the process of creation is the emergence of the Wu Xing or 'Five Elemental Processes'. These are born from the various inter-relations of Yin and Yang when they are combined with the motive force of Taiji. If Yin and Yang produce frequency waves then the Wu Xing give those waves direction.

The Wu Xing are known as Fire, Earth, Metal, Water and Wood and they combine into a cycle of generation and control as shown in Figure 1.13.

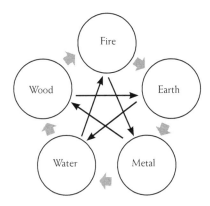

Figure 1.13 The Wu Xing or Five Elemental Processes

The generation cycle (thick grey arrow) shows how one energetic movement can produce another and in this way they produce a perfect and unbroken cycle. This is reflected within nature by the various processes that take place over time, for example, the seasons, the ageing process, etc. These are pure manifestations of the Wu Xing within the physical world. They bring about the concept of constant change and development which are the core principles behind Daoism and their arts.

Table 1.1 shows how changing processes are attached to the Wu Xing. From this chart we can see how the Wu Xing give us change, development, seasons, direction, time, etc. There is an infinite number of categories which could be put into this table; these are just a few examples.

Table 1.1 Categorisation According to Wu Xing

	Fire	Earth	Metal	Water	Wood
Season	Summer	Late summer	Autumn	Winter	Spring
Direction	South	Centre	West	North	East
Climate	Hot	Damp	Dry	Cold	Windy
Emotion	Excitation	Worry	Sadness	Fear	Anger
Colour	Red	Yellow	White	Blue	Green
Time	Morning	Afternoon	Evening	Night	Dawn
Growth	Fruiting	Harvesting	Withering	Dying	Sprouting
Age	Childhood	Adulthood	Old age	Death	Birth

Without the Wu Xing there would be no change, development or progression.

The generation cycle shows the perfect transition from one elemental process to another whereas the controlling cycle (black arrows in the centre of the diagram) shows how one element can inhibit and manage the growth of another. For example, Water generates Wood but it is controlled by Earth and at the same time it controls Fire. This keeps the elements in balance and makes sure that one does not become too strong. One slight alteration and this delicate relationship is thrown out of balance.

The elements are best thought of as five movements which can take place within both the physical and the energetic realm. They are a further combination of Yin and Yang and as such can transfer and change the various vibrational frequencies. Much of Daoist meditation is aimed at gaining a practical understanding of how all of this takes place within the universe, the mind and the body.

Table 1.2 summarises the five movements which are attributed to the elements. The chart begins with the 'Fire' elemental process and ends in 'Wood' but in practice they would continually be cycling from 'Wood' back to 'Fire' and so on. In this way the cycle is ongoing.

Table 1.2 Movement of the Wu Xing

Element	Fire	Earth	Metal	Water	Wood
Movement	Expansion	Division	Contraction	Sinking down	Shooting forward

So, within nature the cycle of energetic movement expands, then it begins to divide into parts, these parts then contract into the centre, then sink downwards to a point before shooting forwards at a high speed. The velocity of this fast shooting forwards movement creates enough kinetic energy for expansion to take place again and the cycle restarts. We can see from this that the fast, shooting forwards motion of the Wood element provides the power for the cycle to take place. For this reason, Wood is usually associated with the catalyst for progress and development, growth, beginnings and birth. Understanding this concept in any more than a scholarly manner requires an advanced knowledge of inner vision through meditation.

The final stage in the Daoist process of creation is the emergence of Heaven and Earth which are represented by a circle divided horizontally into two halves (Figure 1.14)

Heaven is white as it is Yang energy. Earth is Yin and so is shown in black. In creation this is the point when the Earth came into being. Up until now there has been various vibrations and energetic

Figure 1.14 Tian (Heaven) and Di (Earth)

movements due to Yin, Yang and the Wu Xing but now there has been the formation of the physical realm for these energetic movements to take place within. Up until now there was the potential for physicality, change, seasons, etc. but now is the point in the process when these things come into existence and move purely from the energetic realm into the physical.

'The nameless Dao is the origin of Heaven and Earth,

The named gives birth to the myriad things.'

Heaven and Earth each generate their own vibrational frequencies which are constant lines of Yang and Yin respectively. There are no fluctuations or variations in these frequencies. These are represented by the Gua of Qian and Kun. It is difficult to understand how no fluctuations whatsoever could produce a wave as surely this relies on there being opposition and both Yin and Yang to produce the peaks and troughs. In order to experience and understand this you need to have reached a high level of attainment within Nei Gong. At this stage you can experience the pure stillness of Yin and pure movement of Yang as the two energies enter your body and meet in the Dan Tien. This is explained in depth later in Chapter 3.

Figure 1.15 Qian Gua, Pure Yang, Representative of Heaven

Figure 1.16 Kun Gua, Pure Yin, Representative of Earth

THE DAOIST PROCESS OF CREATION

The process of development and transformation which is outlined above is known within the Daoist community as the 'Daoist process of creation' and it is summarised in the diagram shown in Figure 1.17.

REVERSING THE PROCESS

The basic principle of Daoism is to return to the source of all. This was laid down as a principle in the *Dao De Jing* and all Nei Gong practice and Daoist meditation such as internal alchemy follow this rule.

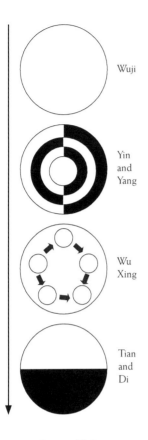

Wuji

Yin and Yang

Wu Xing

Tian and Di

Figure 1.17 The Daoist Process of Creation

The reason for this concept is simple. Everything in the universe originated from emptiness which we call Wuji. Wuji originated from Dao which is what we are aiming for in our practice. We are trying to reunite with Dao and so gain enlightenment. As you can see from the process of creation which we have talked about, several stages have been moved through to take us from emptiness to the divide of Heaven and Earth. This process within the universe is known as the macrocosm. We cannot change this process as we have little control over the macrocosm when we first begin our training but we do have the possibility of taking control of our selves, the microcosm. This is often called the 'inner universe' in Daoism and an identical process of creation takes place within both our physical body and our energy body.

Within the body, this is the process of development we go through in the womb which nine months later culminates in our birth. We obviously cannot reverse this process so we must find another way to go back to the source within our inner universe. That method is reversal of the process of creation that takes place within our energy system. If we can return to the source then we can rediscover our original self prior to the creation of own personal false reality. We can reunite our consciousness with the blank canvas of Wuji prior to Yin and Yang creating distortions which later formed our external persona.

Dao

Gives birth to

Consciousness

Which gives birth to

Existence

Or alternatively

The Realm of Consciousness

Gives birth to

The Energetic Realm

Which gives birth to

The Physical Realm

At an advanced level, our Nei Gong practice is a method of going back through this process. According to Daoist thought, only the realm of consciousness was everlasting and so if we can return to here then we would become immortal. Our spirit would live on whilst our physical shell ceased to exist. A lofty aim indeed! For the many people who wish simply to improve their health, well-being and mental clarity, Nei Gong practice is ideal; these are all benefits which can be had through Nei Gong training.

At first the philosophy of Daoism may seem complicated but as you move through the various stages of practice in this book you will see that the philosophy and the practice are one entity. Through training in Nei Gong you gain an experiential understanding of the very essence of Daoist thought.

CHAPTER 2

THE THREE BODIES OF MAN

To the ancient Daoists, existence was a multi-faceted network of inter-related energies. Rather than restricting their view of life to the three-dimensional, physical world with which Western thought usually concerns itself, Daoists attempt to understand and work with the subtle elements of existence which sit within various overlapping realms. At first this way of understanding life can be confusing, particularly to Westerners, but gaining a better understanding of how the Daoists view the world will help to speed up the progression of your Nei Gong practice.

We have already looked at the Daoist process of creation in the previous chapter. This can help us to understand the formation of the external universe or macrocosm. Now we need to learn how this process is reflected within the microcosm of our own body. This theory is of key importance within any of the Daoist internal arts.

The entity which we simply know as Dao gave birth first to Heaven and then Earth. Within the macrocosm these provided the building blocks for physical existence: a screen upon which the various dramas of life could be projected. Within the microcosm of the human body Dao first gave birth to pure human consciousness which in turn provided the seed for the physical form of our body. Figure 2.1 shows how these two processes directly reflect each other.

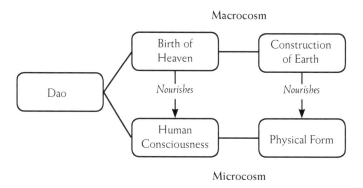

Figure 2.1 Formation of the Microcosm and Macrocosm

The creation of the physical body from Dao takes place prior to our birth. As we grow and develop within the womb, the vibrational frequency of the Dao alters to that of the energetic realm and then from here into the frequency of physical matter. The result of this conversion of energetic substances is the creation of a person: a person made up of three main 'bodies' which were created at the different stages of conversion inherent within human development. These bodies are known as: the consciousness body, the energy body and the physical body.

THE PHYSICAL BODY

The physical body is the body which is easiest for most people to 'feel'. Our physical sense functions are the main connection we have with the outside world and so we learn from an early age to rely heavily on these senses to interact with our world. Our physical body is made up of all of the various tissues, organs, bones and body fluids, etc. with which Western anatomy is concerned. This is the body of form, of construct and physical matter. It is usually the only one of the three bodies of man which can be seen and felt by anybody who has not developed their senses through some form of internal training.

The various parts of the physical body all vibrate from the organs and cells right through to the smallest particles which form our physical building blocks. Although these frequencies differ, they all exist within the scale of the physical realm even though some of these particles may be far too small for us to feel or see.

The physical body exists because of one of the three main energetic substances of man which the Daoists named Jing or 'essence'.

The vibrational frequency of Jing is the furthest from the frequency of the Dao and so Jing sits on the borderline of the physical realm. It vibrates at a similar frequency to the energy of the planet and is considered within Daoist thought to be the substance of nourishment, creation and birth.

THE ENERGY BODY

The energy body sits between the physical body and human consciousness. It is usually completely invisible to those who have not reached an accomplished level in the internal arts and for that reason is usually overlooked within Western concepts of health and existence. It is comprised of innumerable channels and pathways of energy which we know as meridians. These energetic pathways transfer the energy known as Qi throughout the human body to our organs and tissues. It would be impossible to map out the entire human energy body due to its complexity but we can identify and work with some of the major meridians which are commonly used within therapeutic treatments like acupuncture and shiatsu.

The energy body is also comprised of the several energetic fields which expand around the human body; these are collectively known as our aura or Etheric field. The size and density of these fields depends upon our health and level of spiritual attainment.

The final part of the energy body is the three energy centres we know as the Dan Tien. These are very important to Nei Gong practice and a great deal of our work is concerned with the cultivation and development of the three Dan Tien.

Qi vibrates at a higher frequency than Jing and so is further from the physical realm. Qi moves throughout all of our meridian system as well as the external environment. It can be categorised into several main types but for the purposes of Nei Gong practice we only need concern ourselves with the fact that Qi moves within our meridians.

THE CONSCIOUSNESS BODY

The consciousness body is very close to the energy of the Dao. It is the first body of man to develop when we are conceived and the last part of us to remain when we die. It is neither tangible nor logical to understand as it does not conform to the rules of the three-dimensional realm. Trying to pinpoint the location for our consciousness body is impossible as it does not have a tangible structure. To access the consciousness body we have to be able to work with the various layers of our own mind.

The consciousness body is made up of the substance known as Shen or 'spirit' within Daoism. Shen vibrates at a very high frequency and is even further from the physical realm than Qi. The amount of Shen we are able to generate and cultivate will dictate our connection with Dao. A person with a great deal of Shen will be able to access the information of the ancient lineages whilst a person with little Shen will forever be connected purely to the physical world of matter.

JING, QI AND SHEN

It is unlikely that you will ever read any Daoist writings that do not mention the three substances of Jing, Qi and Shen. These three energetic substances control various aspects of our health, nature and psyche as well as our spiritual development.

The key to understanding the nature and functions of Jing, Qi and Shen is understanding one simple fact. They are all manifestations of the same thing. The energy of the Dao is the source for all three substances and they can be compared to the three states of steam, water and ice. Shen is like steam, it is an ethereal vapour that has no form or substance. It can fill any space and is completely free in nature. Despite this it is has the potential for physical substance if it is cooled as it will begin to change into water which can be likened to Qi. Water is also fluid and free but it requires a vessel to flow through or fill. It is more tangible than steam but still extremely fluid and free. If the water is frozen then it will change into ice which can be likened to Jing.

The analogy above can help us understand how the three substances are really one and how they can change from one form to another. It is more accurate to look at them as three vibrational frequencies which can either become higher or lower. As the frequency is changed, the substances transform from one form to another as shown in Figure 2.2.

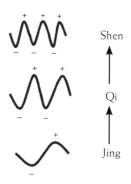

Figure 2.2 Jing, Qi and Shen Transformation

In the Daoist process of creation, the energy of Dao is gradually taken down through the various steps which create the physical realm. In this way Dao changes to Shen, Qi, Jing and finally physical matter. This process continues until all of our energy is spent, our Jing begins to deplete and then finally we die.

Through Nei Gong practice this is where we begin to reverse the natural course and so head back towards the source. We use our practice to convert Jing back to Qi, Shen and finally the energy of Dao. This enables us to attain a spiritual awakening.

Imbalances of Awareness

The human mind is the source of our thoughts and intentions. Our awareness leads us to carry out the various functions which are necessary to live our daily lives. It is 'tuned in to' the frequency of the physical realm as this is the world in which we find ourselves. Our senses dictate the majority of our actions and help us to touch, taste, see, smell and hear the outside world. For this reason we can say that the majority of our awareness is usually 'tuned in to' the physical body.

The human mind can, like a radio, tune in to the frequencies of the energy body and consciousness body if it is trained enough through a practice such as Nei Gong. This is when we start to develop an internal awareness of the movement of Qi and eventually Shen.

All of us can already feel the movements of Qi and Shen to varying degrees. The changes and fluctuations of energy within the three bodies of man create external manifestations which are clear for us to feel. The movements of Qi and Shen create the emotions which we look at in more detail later in this chapter (see pages 51–53). Emotions are like waves on an ocean; our consciousness is like the wind. As the wind of our consciousness blows, waves are created within the energy body which move across the ocean of our mind. These waves are transitory and constantly changing according to the direction and intensity of the wind.

Our mind will tend to have a preoccupation with one or more of the three bodies of man as well as tuning in to the wants and needs of the physical sense functions. This preoccupation creates an imbalance within our awareness which creates one of the following problems.

Preoccupation with the Physical Body
A person preoccupied with the functions of the physical body will be entirely attached to the physical realm. They will be fairly unaware of their emotions and often seen by others to be devoid of any feelings or sensitivity. They will usually be guided by physical desires and wants such as the base needs for food and sex. The problem with this kind of preoccupation is that it speeds up the conversion of the energetic substances into Jing and then the depletion of Jing, especially through sexual activities. Jing sits on the border of the physical realm; as its vibrational frequency lowers and it moves into the physical realm it is converted into several main tangible substances including semen and sexual fluid. Excessive sexual activity depletes the Jing and so drains the body of its essence. At the same time, the desire for physical gratification increases and so more Jing is converted into sexual fluid ready for use. In this way a vicious cycle is created and sexual addiction or rather addiction to the wants of the physical body is created. Preoccupation with the physical body tends to be more prevalent in younger people and then men throughout the rest of their lives. It is in a woman's nature to move into a preoccupation with the energy body although this is not a hard and fast rule.

Preoccupation with the Energy Body
The energy body is most easily felt through the movements of the emotions. A person who is preoccupied with the functions of the energy body will be too attached to their emotional states, unfortunately it is often the case that people attach to the more negative emotions and so sink into spiralling states of depression and sadness or anger.

Excessive attachment to the emotions can start to disperse the Qi which means that we have less vitality which results in sickness. It is interesting to note that in the case of extremely stressful situations, a person may suddenly find that they become numb and devoid of any emotional response whatsoever. Western thought would say that the person is in shock whilst Daoist thought says that the mind has switched its preoccupation to the physical body in order to protect itself from dispersal of Qi.

Preoccupation with the energy body is more natural for women than men although this trend is changing in modern times as the divide between the Yin energy of women and the Yang energy of man is beginning to lessen.

Preoccupation with the Consciousness Body

The consciousness body is the furthest from the physical realm and so usually the hardest body for our mind to 'tune in to' but some individuals have this problem. To these people the physical world can seem like something very far away. They are dreamlike and trapped within the constantly emerging thoughts which fill their mind. It is common for this to lead to some sort of mental illness as the energy of the Dao is not very far from their mind at any time. Meditation is one way of preparing a person's mind prior to attaining union with the Dao, as well as helping to refine the substances of Jing, Qi and Shen; it also provided a safeguard against the practitioner going insane.

Within Nei Gong training we wish to seek out a balance between the three bodies of man and allow our mind to naturally develop a healthy awareness of all three. This is why our practice works first with the physical body, then the energy body and, only when the time is right, the consciousness body. Skipping stages runs the risk of developing an imbalance in our awareness.

CONNECTION OF THE THREE BODIES OF MAN

The three bodies are connected as shown in Figure 2.3.

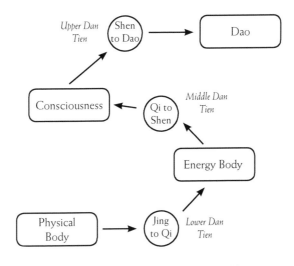

Figure 2.3 Connection of the Three Bodies via the Dan Tien

The three Dan Tien are key elements within both the transformation of Jing to Qi to Shen and also the connection of the three bodies.

Jing is the raw essence of creation which is closest to the physical realm. It is actually stored around the kidney area of the body and then passed into the lower Dan Tien.

The lower Dan Tien is a sphere of energy which sits inside the lower abdomen below the navel. It is roughly two inches across in most adult humans although this can vary from person to person. It has several uses which we will look at later (see pages 65–67) but one of its most important roles is that of converting our Jing to Qi. Over the course of a day, some of our Jing moves downwards from the kidney area into the sexual organs for conversion into sexual fluid, more Jing moves into the lower Dan Tien where it is gradually transformed into Qi. The movement and transformation of Jing means that the frequency of the wave increases and so the substance moves further from the physical realm into purely the energetic. As this happens, the information contained within the Jing will be translated by the body as a gentle heat. If conversion of Jing to Qi is taking place naturally and healthily then a person will have a constantly warm lower abdomen. In babies and young children this process is taking place at a faster rate to assist in their growth and development and so they should always have a warm belly.

As the Qi is created within the lower Dan Tien it is directed into the meridian system and so helps to nourish the energy body. For this reason we can say that the lower Dan Tien is like a gateway which enables us to access the energy system. It is for this reason that in the earliest stages of Nei Gong training we spend a lot of time focusing our mind on the lower Dan Tien; this helps to generate more Qi as well as tune the mind in to the frequency of the meridians system. Problems arise if this process is carried on for too long; if we focus on the lower Dan Tien for too many years past this process being complete we will begin to alter the natural state of the mind and so develop an excessive preoccupation with the energy body as described above. We will then become trapped by the movement of our emotions and so begin to develop what the ancient Daoists named 'dragon sickness' or 'Qi Gong sickness'. Do not worry though, we will talk about when to end each stage in your training and cover what signs there are to tell you when you have finished working with the lower Dan Tien.

Qi is moved into various parts of the energy body including the middle Dan Tien which is our second ball of energy; it sits at the level of the heart in the centre of our chest. Here the Qi is refined and so turned into Shen, the energy of our consciousness body. As the Qi moves and transforms in this area we can feel a deep vibration move through the body which is the feeling translated by the body from the information contained within the Qi. We can see from this how our middle Dan Tien is the gateway to the consciousness body.

The final stage of transformation takes place within the upper Dan Tien which sits at the level of our forehead. This is the conversion of Shen to the pure emptiness of Dao. The information at this stage in the transformation is translated as light by the mind and so we can often see a bright white or golden light within our head or sometimes glowing around our head in the form of a halo. Many spiritual traditions including Christianity talk about this white light and link it to spiritual growth. You only have to walk into any church to see the images of saints surrounded by halos on the stained glass windows.

THE MYSTERIOUS PASS

Daoists placed great importance upon a place known as the mysterious pass. The mysterious pass was first mentioned within the *Dao De Jing* some 2500 years ago by Laozi and so was one of the original principles of Daoist philosophy. It is the point from which the source of creation can be found and human enlightenment can be brought forth if only we can settle our mind here.

> *'It is the most profound principle that there exists an enigmatic process,*
>
> *It is born forth from the mysterious pass.'*

Rather than being a physical location on the body (which is a common misunderstanding) the mysterious pass is found when the mind rests equally between the three bodies of man. It is at this point that none of the preoccupations mentioned earlier are present and so awareness is balanced between the three bodies of man as shown in Figure 2.4.

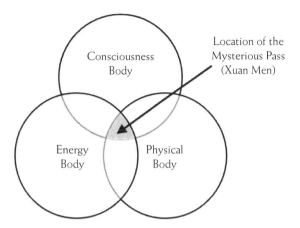

Figure 2.4 The Three Bodies of Man and the Mysterious Pass

Balance between the bodies can only be achieved once the condition of the three bodies has been improved and they are functioning in a healthy and efficient manner. This stage of attainment is not required until much later in your Nei Gong training. This is the point at which your Nei Gong has begun to merge with meditation. For now it is enough to understand the reason for the union of the three bodies of man.

THE ENERGY BODY

At this point it is worth looking at the components of the energy body in further detail as a great deal of Nei Gong practice is concerned with awakening and working with the various elements of your meridian system.

The energy body can be divided into three main parts. The acquired components, the congenital components and miscellaneous components.

Acquired Components of the Energy Body

- The Fire Element Meridians

- The Earth Element Meridians

- The Metal Element Meridians

- The Water Element Meridians

- The Wood Element Meridians

Congenital Components of the Energy Body

- The Congenital Meridians

- The Three Dan Tien

Miscellaneous Components of the Energy Body

- The Wei Qi Field

- The Aura

THE ACQUIRED ENERGY BODY

The acquired components of the energy body are the elements of the energy system which become of prime importance after a person is born. The acquired parts of the energy body are comprised of the 12 meridians which are linked to various organs of the body. These are the meridians largely used within therapies such as acupuncture and shiatsu and the easiest to map out on the body.

Figure 2.5 shows the various pathways of the 12 acquired meridians. If you want more detailed diagrams of the acquired meridians then you should consult any acupuncture text book as these meridians are well documented within Chinese medicine.

Each of the meridians is named after the organ it links to with the exception of the Triple Heater meridian which is named after three separate chambers in the torso which act to regulate and balance the temperatures and internal pressures of the body as well as direct the flow of Qi, blood and body fluids. The pericardium is also treated as an organ in Traditional Chinese Medicine (TCM) when it is in fact a sac which surrounds the heart.

Over the course of our daily lives we accumulate blockages in these meridians due to information being passed directly into our energy body from various factors such as the outside environment and our interaction with other people. These blockages occur at a fairly superficial level within our body and can be cleared easily through internal practices such as Qi Gong and Taiji. It is only if these blockages are left unchecked that over time they build up and can seriously impede Qi flow which can in turn lead to sickness.

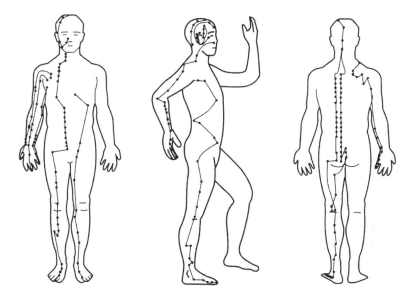

Figure 2.5 The Acquired Meridians

The 12 meridians of the acquired energy body are also grouped under the headings of the Wu Xing as shown in Table 2.1.

Table 2.1 Elemental Associations of the 12 Acquired Meridians

Acquired Meridian	Wu Xing Element
Heart, Small Intestine, Pericardium, Triple Heater	Fire
Spleen, Stomach	Earth
Lung, Large Intestine	Metal
Kidneys, Bladder	Water
Liver, Gallbladder	Wood

The balance of the energy within the 12 acquired meridians can be understood through Wu Xing theory and the diagram shown in Figure 2.6.

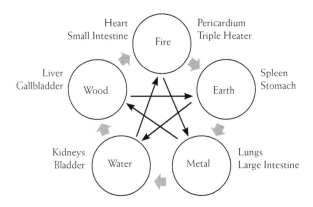

Figure 2.6 Wu Xing Diagram

The theory of Wu Xing shows how delicate the balance between the meridians is. The outside circle is the creation cycle which shows how the energy of one element creates the next. The central 'star shaped' arrangement of arrows is the controlling cycle; this shows how the energy of one element keeps another in check by preventing it from growing too large. Wu Xing theory within Chinese medicine is both complex and immensely deep. It is also well documented and for this reason we will not look at it in any more detail within this book. It is more important that I cover material which is not so well understood in the West.

Circulation of Qi takes place from the lower Dan Tien which rotates to direct the movement of Qi much like a water wheel. As the Qi moves into various meridians and organs it takes on various properties according to which organ it passes through. The quality of the Qi is then changed so that it can carry out one of several different functions. It is useful for Nei Gong training to have knowledge of the qualities of the five main different types of Qi that move through our acquired meridian system and how they affect us when they are in an imbalanced state.

Imbalances and blockages in the meridians of the energy body will have an effect on both the physical and the consciousness bodies which will vary according to whether the imbalance is due to an excess or a deficiency of elemental Qi.

BALANCING THE FIRE ELEMENTAL MERIDIANS

Fire elemental Qi is an expansive energy that spreads warmth out in all directions when it is in balance. It is housed primarily within the heart but travels through the meridians of the heart, pericardium and small intestine as well as the Triple Heater system.

The Qi from this area of the body also radiates outside of our body. It is easy to feel people who have a healthy balance of Fire Qi as they have a warm and healthy glow about them.

An excessive amount of Fire Qi will expand in an erratic and 'sputtering' fashion which has the effect of producing hysteria and slightly manic behaviour within a person's consciousness. They will often have wild, staring eyes and laugh at inappropriate moments uncontrollably. Physically this excess of energy will manifest as a flushed complexion and a buildup of heat and pressure around the chest area which can manifest as various physical difficulties.

When the Fire Qi is deficient due to blockages within this area of the acquired meridian system a person will find it difficult to heat their body and their circulation will be poor. They will also have difficulty getting excited about anything and lack joy within their lives. People here will have a tendency to struggle with self-pity as the lack of Fire Qi means that they will become swallowed up in an excess of Metal Qi which is linked to feelings of hopelessness and depression.

As you progress through your Nei Gong training you are likely to feel the effects of your energy within the acquired meridian system moving into a balanced state. The emotional fluctuations described above will slowly begin to be replaced by a feeling of contentment which is far more permanent and steady.

BALANCING THE EARTH ELEMENTAL MERIDIANS

Earth elemental Qi is housed primarily within the spleen but is circulated through the meridians of both the spleen and the stomach; it is the energy of change and development.

Excessive Earth Qi will cause a person to 'over-think' about external factors and worry intensely about every little event. The Earth elemental Qi will begin to stagnate and feel stodgy within the meridians which causes the lower part of the body to swell as the conversion of Jing to Qi is compromised. Physical problems will usually arise within the stomach quickly once the Earth elemental Qi is imbalanced. It is interesting to note that a person's external energy field (aura) has a thick viscous feel to it when the Earth elemental Qi is in excess.

A deficiency of Earth elemental Qi becomes internally directed, so a person starts to worry about their own actions. They will find the natural progression and development which is a part of life difficult to deal with and they will begin to stagnate: an effect which is commonly known as 'being stuck in a rut'. The spleen becomes compromised and we begin to experience an increase in self-doubt and worry. Overly strong introspection is usually linked to a deficient amount of Qi within the Earth elemental meridians.

As the energy within these meridians becomes balanced and blockages clear, self-doubt begins to vanish and external events cease to worry us anymore. This is extremely healthy for us if we wish to move through life and achieve our full potential. Daoism is very much concerned with personal development and spiritual elevation so the balancing of our earth elemental Qi is of the utmost importance.

BALANCING THE METAL ELEMENTAL MERIDIANS

The Metal elemental Qi is housed within the lungs although it also travels through the large intestine meridian. Metal Qi is the energy of contraction which when balanced can feel like a reassuring hug but when imbalanced can feel constrictive and suffocating.

When Metal elemental Qi is in excess we can experience heightened feelings of sadness and grief. This deep depression becomes outwardly manifested and so is very draining for those around you. The contracting movement of the Qi acts as a type of magnet which literally drains Qi from the nearby environment or other people. It is common for people to experience a feeling of exhaustion when they have spent time around a person who is living with depression. This is primarily due to the effect of the contracting Metal elemental Qi.

A deficiency of Metal elemental Qi also leads to feelings of sadness and depression but the feeling is more internally directed much like falling into a deep dark hole. The person may well feel isolated from the rest of the world and their external senses.

As Metal elemental Qi begins to become balanced we are less likely to experience feelings of despair and hopelessness which enables us to see external events from a far more objective perspective.

BALANCING THE WATER ELEMENTAL MERIDIANS

The Water elemental Qi is housed within the kidneys. It travels through the kidney and bladder meridians. Water Qi is quite versatile and changes its properties depending on whether it is excess or deficiency. Excessive Water elemental Qi spirals upwards like a natural spring forcing its way through the rocks. A person with this excess of Qi will live with a constant feeling of panic and paranoia, their nervous system is always running on full and they become very highly strung. This can result in an energetic burnout which leads to all sorts of illnesses linked to our vitality and energy levels.

A deficiency of Water elemental Qi results in a feeling of inner fear and shyness which results from the Qi slowly sinking down within the body. The world will seem like a big and scary place; they will live with constant fear.

As our Water elemental Qi moves into balance our kidneys become stronger which is extremely important within Nei Gong training as we discuss in Chapter 6 (see pages 148–152). We are less likely to be affected by our own fears and we will suffer far less stress and tension in the course of our daily lives.

BALANCING THE WOOD ELEMENTAL MERIDIANS

Wood elemental Qi is housed within the liver and travels through both the liver and the gallbladder meridians. It is a straightforward elemental energy which travels in a very direct manner.

An excess of Wood elemental Qi causes a person to experience outbursts of frustration and anger which are usually directed into the external environment and the people around them. This is a destructive energy for both the sufferer and the other people in their lives.

A deficiency of Wood elemental Qi is equally as destructive as the hatred and frustration is directed inwards resulting in a feeling of worthlessness.

As the Wood elemental Qi moves into balance we will find a feeling of inner calm and patience which enables us to function well within even the most stressful situations.

ACCESSING THE CONSCIOUSNESS BODY

We have already talked about how the middle Dan Tien is the 'gateway' to the consciousness body. This is the area where our awareness may access the subtle vibrational frequency of the layers of Shen which relate directly to the functioning of our innate nature. We can picture the middle Dan Tien as the gateway and the various emotional fluctuations of the Wu Xing as the locks on the gate. Only if we are able to balance our elemental Qi and so our transient emotions will we be able to work with our consciousness. This is possibly the most difficult part of Nei Gong training as the emotions are very difficult elements to bring into balance since we are subjected to their movements and changes on a daily basis.

THE CONGENITAL ENERGY BODY

The congenital energy body is primarily made up of the eight congenital meridians which are also known as the extra-ordinary meridians. The remainder of the congenital energy body is made up of the three rotating energy centres which we know as Dan Tien.

The congenital meridians differ from the acquired meridians in several ways. First, they are not directly linked to any of the organs. Although they have an effect on the health of the physical body, they are more to do with circulation and transmutation of Jing, Qi and Shen. If we wish to develop spiritually then it is the congenital meridians that we need to work with.

Usually within Chinese medicine theory they talk about the congenital meridians being like 'reservoirs' of Qi. This Qi is then passed down into the acquired meridians for use by the organs. When there is an abundance of energy moving through the acquired meridians, the congenital meridians draw this excess away and store it until everything naturally moves back into balance. This happens as first the Yin and Yang linking meridians make sure that there is an even flow of Qi across the related meridians within the body. Every acquired meridian can be separated into Yin and Yang. The Yin linking meridian connects each of the Yin meridians and the Yang linking meridian connects all of the Yang meridians. If the regulation of Qi across the Yin and Yang meridians is not enough to deal with an excess of energy then it is drawn away by the Yin and Yang heel meridians. It is moved into the thrusting and girdling meridians where it is stored. The purpose of the governing and conception meridians is to then circulate it around the body and allow it to move back into the acquired meridians as it is required. In this manner the congenital meridians work as a sort of Qi irrigation system.

NEI GONG THEORY OF THE CONGENITAL MERIDIANS

Within the womb we do not rely heavily upon the acquired meridians which are the last part of our energy system to develop. Instead we use the congenital meridians which come into being alongside the three Dan Tien.

The movement of Qi within our congenital meridians is very strong and this gives us the necessary internal force for creation and development prior to being born. The Dan Tien rotate steadily and push the Jing, Qi and Shen through our newly formed physical body as we begin to become aware of our sensing functions and relationship with the outside world and, most importantly, our mother. Figure 2.7 shows the pathway of the congenital meridians within a foetus.

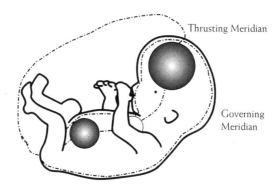

Figure 2.7 The Human Foetus

After we are born, we begin to use our acquired meridians to a far greater degree and gradually the movement of Qi within the congenital meridians begins to slow down. As our growth begins to slow down we do not need such a strong rotation of the lower Dan Tien and so by the time we reach our mid teens the turning of the lower Dan Tien has slowed to almost a crawl and there is little movement of Qi within the congenital meridians. It is at this time that they begin to function in the manner described above, as reservoirs of Qi.

The problem with this is that the movement of Qi within our congenital meridians does not only control the speed of our growth and physical development but also our ability to learn and develop spiritually. The transportation of Shen to the mind slows dramatically and after another decade or so our ability to learn has been reduced. From the second we are born we are subjected to the outside influences of the world and other people which begin to develop our 'false sense of self' known as the Ego and our emotions begin to govern us. The movement of Qi being slowed allows blockages and imbalances to develop at a higher rate and so our physical health is affected. We gradually begin to develop a buildup of negative Qi which is likely to lead to illness in later life.

If, however, we are able to reawaken the Dan Tien and begin to restore movement of Qi within the congenital meridians then we will be able to restart this process of internal change and development which is the key to spiritual advancement.

The majority of Daoist literature talks about the 'small water wheels' of Qi which are also known as the 'small circulations' or the

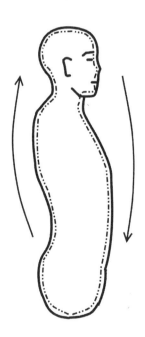

'micro-cosmic orbits'. These are several circulations of energy which take place within the congenital energy body once you have restored Qi movement through the rotation of the lower Dan Tien. In the majority of cases, Daoist books will talk only of the circulation that takes place up the governing meridian and down the conception meridian as shown in Figure 2.8.

This is usually the only small water wheel of Qi mentioned since it is the circulation relevant to Daoist meditation practices. Within the internal arts such as Nei Gong we need to start the rest of the small water wheels which surround the body. Once we have done this we will

Figure 2.8 The Ren and Du Small Water Wheel of Qi

have encased our energy body within a type of 'energetic cage' which serves to create enough internal force to start the large water wheel of Qi which is also known as the 'macro-cosmic orbit'. Figure 2.9 shows the energetic cage formed by the small water wheels of Qi.

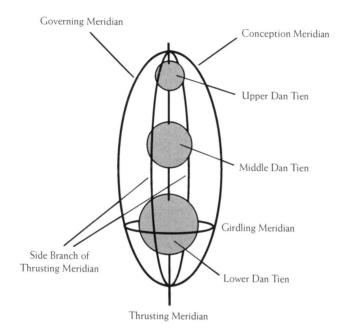

Figure 2.9 The Energetic Cage of the Small Water Wheels of Qi

It is at this stage that we are able to fully integrate the energy body into the physical body and so circulate Qi and eventually Shen throughout our entire system. If we can do this then we are said to have achieved a 'congenital state of being'. This is the key to health and longevity through Nei Gong practice.

THE GOVERNING AND CONCEPTION MERIDIANS
The governing meridian runs up the back of the body whilst the conception meridian runs down the front as shown in Figure 2.10. Qi naturally moves up the back of the body and down the front through the circuit formed by these two meridians.

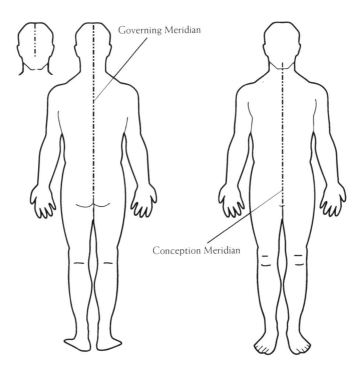

Figure 2.10 The Governing and Conception Meridians

The basic purpose of Qi circulation along these meridians is to bring fresh energy to each of the acquired organ meridians which takes a total of 24 hours for one circulation. This is due to the speed of the Dan Tien, which in the majority of people turns only once each day.

If we are able to restore a healthier level of Qi movement in these meridians through our practice and start the first 'small water wheel of Qi' this process will takes place faster and more efficiently meaning that the organs receive more Qi. The Qi will then also be led into the bones and most importantly the bone marrow through the spine which also connects to the brain. The Daoists called this 'marrow and brain cleaning' and this was an important part of their practices. Attaining this level of energetic circulation helps in the healthy production of red and white blood cells as well as improving the various functions of the brain and our learning capacity.

THE THRUSTING MERIDIAN

The thrusting meridian has several branches which run throughout the body as shown in Figure 2.11.

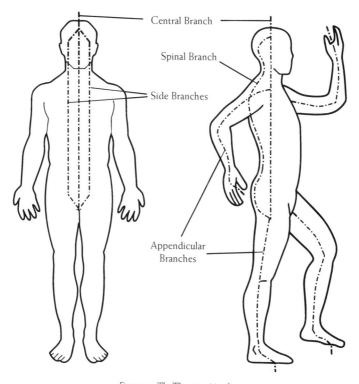

Figure 2.11 The Thrusting Meridian

The thrusting meridian has one main branch which runs through the centre of the spinal cord. This is usually the part of the thrusting meridian which is talked about within Chinese medicine texts. A second branch runs from the crown of the head at a point called Baihui (GV20) down to the Huiyin (CV1) point which sits at our perineum. There are also two side branches which extend through our torso and finally four branches which run down the centre of the arms and legs.

The thrusting meridian connects the three Dan Tien and is the primary vessel for transporting the three substances of Jing, Qi and Shen once they have been converted within the three Dan Tien. It is deep within these meridians that we are often able to experience the movement of these three substances during meditative practices such as internal alchemy.

The majority of people have very little movement of Qi within these channels, in particular the side branches and the meridian that runs from the crown to the perineum.

Once we are able to restore movement to the energy which is running through these meridians we will have started several more 'small water wheels' of Qi. These circulations are extremely important for us if we wish to achieve any sort of spiritual awakening. They help to divide the forces of Yin and Yang within the body and create two strong energetic poles which enable the movement of Shen along the 'large water wheel' of Qi.

THE GIRDLING MERIDIAN

The girdling meridian is unique in that it is the only meridian to run horizontally through the body if we are standing up. It has several functions and pathways but the main location of the girdling meridian is shown in Figure 2.12.

The girdling meridian is very important in the process of awakening the lower Dan Tien as it forms a sort of energetic 'vortex' which enwraps the lower Dan Tien area. Much like a kind of gyroscope, the circulation of Qi in the girdling meridian helps to direct and turn the lower Dan Tien in various directions. You will see from Figure 2.12 that the girdling meridian has a slight downwards dip as it moves from the rear to the front of the body. This is so that Qi moves towards the front of the body and gives the lower Dan Tien the correct impetus to rotate forward, the direction required for the most important circulation of Qi which runs up the governing meridian and down the conception meridian.

Figure 2.12 The Girdling Meridian

The other main branches of the girdling meridian which are not usually included within internal arts books are the branches which coil in either direction out of the girdling meridian and entwine around the body as shown in Figure 2.13.

These coils of energy can be felt very clearly once you have managed to circulate Qi through the girdling meridian. It is often the case that your body will begin to sway and turn as shown in Figure 2.14 as the spiralling branches open up and direct Qi around the outside of your body.

When the coils are working efficiently, you will have managed to turn the body into a kind of internal energy magnet. The Daoists called this stage the attainment of Hunyuan, which can be translated as meaning 'mixed rotations' or sometimes simply 'primordial'. It is the method through which the force of Taiji contained within your body reacts with the energy of the external environment.

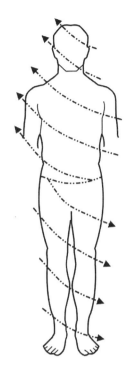

Figure 2.13 The Energetic Coil of the Girdling Meridian

THE YIN AND YANG LINKING MERIDIANS

The Yin and Yang linking meridians have been mentioned briefly already. They run down the body as shown in Figure 2.15.

The job of the Yin and Yang linking meridians is to ensure that an even amount of Qi runs through all of the acquired meridians. If there is an excess or deficiency within any one meridian then they help to redistribute the Qi to make it even. Only when the level is even across the acquired meridians is any excess Qi taken back into the congenital meridians.

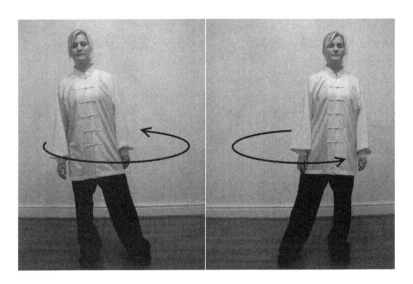

Figure 2.14 Reacting to the Spiralling Qi

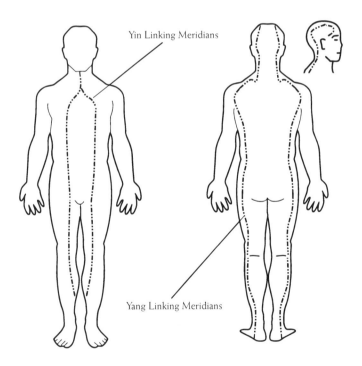

Yin Linking Meridians

Yang Linking Meridians

Figure 2.15 The Yin and Yang Linking Meridians

THE YIN AND YANG HEEL MERIDIANS

The Yin and Yang heel meridians are extremely important within the energy body. They serve as a type of energetic fuse which ensures that extreme excesses of Qi are drawn away from the body and down into the earth. They are shown in Figure 2.16.

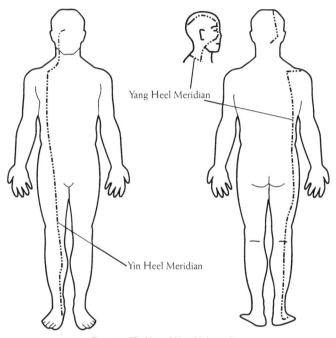

Yang Heel Meridian

Yin Heel Meridian

Figure 2.16 The Yin and Yang Heel Meridians

The Yang heel meridian draws excess Qi down away from the head to prevent it damaging your mind. In the case of serious meditation practitioners, the Yang heel meridian carries out the same function with Shen. If you develop your Shen too quickly and send it up to the mind then it can lead to mental illness. The Yang heel meridian prevents this from happening.

The Yin heel meridian draws excess energy away from the body and in particular the lower abdomen where an excess of Qi can create stagnation and prevent the Dan Tien from rotating efficiently.

These are the two main meridians for helping an internal arts practitioner 'ground' themselves. They are fairly simple to open in comparison to some of the other meridians as a correct standing posture and good alignments will enable them to function properly.

Box 2.1 Sinking Like Water

The Qi which circulates within your body moves in various directions according to the rotation of the lower Dan Tien and the layout of the meridian system. As well as this Qi there is also the Qi which sits within the two main cavities of the body, the thoracic cavity and the abdominal cavity. It is considered better for your health if the flow of Qi within these two chambers flows downwards towards the floor. This Qi is then topped up by the energy drawn into the body when we breathe. If this Qi begins to rise it can lead to an increase in heat which raises the blood pressure and leads to an increase in physical and mental tension. This is obviously damaging to our health in the long run as well as being detrimental to our practice.

'Water makes its way to the lowest places,

The true practitioner should behave like water.'

Your internal Qi should flow gently downwards like water seeping down through cracks in a rock face. This will keep your body relaxed and your mind calm as well as 'earthing you' which many practitioners of Qi Gong consider to be of great importance. What they mean by this is that you are literally increasing your energetic connection to the planet which has a nourishing and balancing effect upon your energy body.

Stand in a neutral position as if you are about to begin the Ji Ben Qi Gong exercises (see Chapter 4). Have your feet a shoulder width apart with your arms hanging by your sides. Ensure that your spine is open and your head feels as though the crown is gently lifting up into the sky. Practise your Sung breathing technique for a short while before beginning to direct the Qi of your body gently down into the floor. Let your mind start at the top of your head and then move down through your torso into your legs. From here continue down into the feet and finally the floor. This process should take a few minutes each time. Do not picture anything in particular. Simply allow your awareness to move down through your body like a wave and this will be enough to lead the Qi in the correct direction. Repeat this as many times as you wish.

It will not be long before you feel your body and mind relax. Your emotions will begin to still and any prior problems will seem far smaller after practising this exercise. It is important that your skeleton does not collapse as this will inhibit Qi and blood flow. Your bones should remain still and aligned whilst your muscles soften.

Practise this exercise as often as you wish. The amount of time is not important. Even a few minutes between other activities is useful. It can also be practised when sitting cross legged on the floor or in a chair.

THE THREE DAN TIEN

The three Dan Tien sit within the body and are connected by the central branch of the thrusting meridian as shown in Figure 2.17.

The Dan Tien are the primary energy centres within the human body that serve to transport the three substances of man and transform them through Nei Gong practice. They also serve as a point through which the mind can access the energy and consciousness bodies.

Each Dan Tien is a sphere of Qi which is held together within a type of energetic/magnetic field formed from the surrounding meridians. The centre point of each Dan Tien is empty and able to fill with Jing, Qi or Shen so that it may be transformed into its next state. This is able to happen due to the nature of the information contained within the vibrational frequency of the Qi which forms each Dan Tien's outer shell.

The three Dan Tien naturally rotate over a 24-hour period on a horizontal axis as shown in Figure 2.18.

A great deal of work within Nei Gong concerns awakening and working with the three Dan Tien; in particular the lower Dan Tien which is the manifestation of Taiji within the body.

THE LOWER DAN TIEN

The lower Dan Tien is the prime driving force for Qi throughout our body. Compared to a water wheel within Daoist literature it pushes Qi through the 'waterways' of our energy body. It is situated roughly three inches below the navel and right in the core of our body. It sits within a triangle of points known as Mingmen (GV4), Huiyin (CV1) and the navel as shown in Figure 2.19.

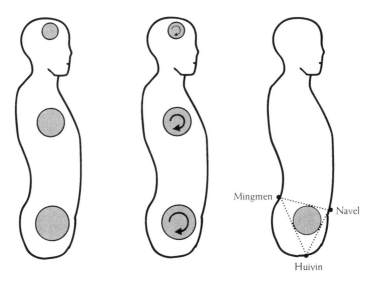

Mingmen

Navel

Huiyin

Figure 2.17 The San Dan Tien *Figure 2.18 Natural* *Figure 2.19 Location of the*
Rotation of the Dan Tien *Lower Dan Tien*

The lower Dan Tien must be rotated more efficiently if we wish to progress within our Nei Gong practice. Many internal arts practitioners miss this fact and it greatly inhibits their development. Trying to practise Nei Gong without creating movement in the lower Dan Tien is like trying to run a large machine on a very small engine. Daoist theory states that for any process to take place we need a catalyst. Within the Daoist process of creation this catalyst was the spiralling force known as Taiji. In order for us to start any energetic process within the microcosm of our body we need to manifest Taiji and the lower Dan Tien is the key.

Many practitioners operate on the idea that we are trying to 'store' Qi within the lower Dan Tien when we practise the internal arts. This actually goes against the teachings of Daoism which state that we should breathe in and out Qi in the same way that we breathe in and out air. Qi that is created within the lower Dan Tien is stored within the congenital meridians as part of a natural process over which we do not need conscious control. Attempting to 'pack' Qi into the lower abdomen will eventually just contribute to stagnation taking place which in turn slows the movement of the Dan Tien and causes the belly to swell. If you get the chance to visit one of the few Daoist monasteries in China or Taiwan that have not been repainted in recent years you will see that many of the statues have Taiji symbols on their lower abdomen as shown in Figure 2.20. This is a demonstration of their attainment of a rotating lower energy centre.

Figure 2.20 Lower Dan Tien Symbol

THE MIDDLE AND UPPER DAN TIEN

The middle Dan Tien sits in the centre of the chest at the same height as the heart as shown in Figure 2.21. It is slightly smaller than the lower Dan Tien but rotates in the same way as it converts Qi to Shen and propels it through the meridians system.

The middle Dan Tien is the connecting 'gateway' between the energy and consciousness bodies. It is the location for the energetic manifestation of the outer layers of the consciousness: the transient emotions. It is from here that the energy of the elemental Qi passes into our mind and affects our false sense of self. All work with the middle Dan Tien is aimed at working with our emotions and sometimes this work can be psychologically difficult. It is advised that a strong foundation in the lower levels of Nei Gong is built before

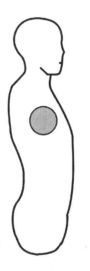

Figure 2.21 The Middle Dan Tien

moving on to this stage. Within my own school it is unusual for any of my students to begin working with the middle Dan Tien until they have completed several years of regular training in the earlier stages of Nei Gong.

The upper Dan Tien sits within the head behind a point known as Yintang as shown in Figure 2.22. The upper Dan Tien is where our Shen is directed after it moves up into our head. From here it is directed into the consciousness body and, if we are advanced enough in our practice, converted into emptiness, the raw essence of the Dao. Advanced work with the upper Dan Tien can be slightly risky if not carried out under supervision by an experienced practitioner. It can lead to the awakening of mental functions which lie dormant within most people which we will discuss further in Chapter 8.

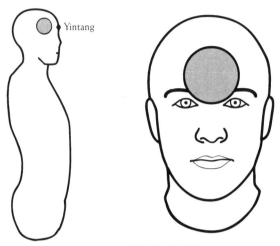

Figure 2.22 The Upper Dan Tien

MISCELLANEOUS COMPONENTS OF THE ENERGY BODY

There are several other parts of the energy body which do not fall directly under the headings of either acquired or congenital. We will look briefly at two of the most important miscellaneous components: the Wei Qi field and the aura.

The Wei Qi Field

The Wei Qi field is the protective shell of Qi which runs around the skin of your entire body as shown in Figure 2.23.

The purpose of the Wei Qi field is to filter out and protect you from incoming negative information. The English translation of Wei Qi field, is 'guardian Qi' field, which sums up its role very well.

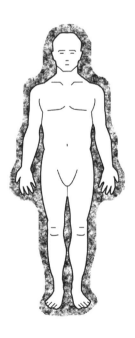

Figure 2.23 The Wei Qi Field

Wei Qi is made up of a combination of Qi from the acquired meridians and Jing from the kidney area of the body and so the quality of your Jing will directly influence the strength of your guardian Qi.

If your guardian Qi is strong it will act as a shield and keep out external pathogens which would result in illness if they were to enter your body. If your guardian Qi is weak then even the slightest drop in temperature can cause Qi stagnation which will make you sick.

What is not so well documented is the second layer of your guardian Qi which deals with emotional information transmission. This layer of guardian Qi expands around us for roughly 12 inches forming an energetic field. Emotional guardian Qi is a combination of Qi and Shen rather than Jing. Emotional information transmission is something that most of us have experienced even if we were not aware of it. When somebody is in a heightened emotional state they can pass this information on to others in the general vicinity. For example, a depressed person may cause their friend to feel depressed also. This is because the emotional guardian Qi layer is weak and so information transmission is passed on. The depressed person is experiencing a sinking of their Qi and this then passes on making the friends Qi sink as well. A strong emotional Qi layer will prevent this from happening.

The Aura (Etheric Body)

The aura or Etheric body is the outer shell of your energetic field which expands like a bubble of Qi around your body as shown in Figure 2.24. The aura is a unique part of your energy system as it serves to store all sorts of information like a great database of binary code.

Life is a series of interactions which takes place not only on a physical level but also within the energetic and consciousness realms. The aura stores Yin and Yang information from these interactions within the Qi which surrounds you. All living creatures

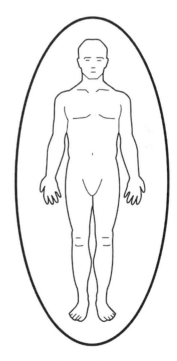

Figure 2.24 The Aura

have this energetic field and without knowing it we begin to draw information from this field the second we move into the vicinity of another person's aura. We have all experienced this reading of another person's aura even if we were not aware of it. Perhaps you met somebody who you instantly liked or had a feeling of distrust from? Many intuitive impressions of another which take place upon meeting them are rooted in your ability to draw information from their energy field. The fact is that most people cannot gain a conscious control of this ability since their intuitive sense is buried deep beneath their Ego (see page 72 for further detail).

Unfortunately we store information from all of the negative events which we have experienced over the course of our lives including traumatic events, abuse, arguments, sicknesses, etc. Over time these pieces of information stick to us and literally weigh us down on an energetic level. Many energetic therapists can feel this clearly when they place their hands on you, as they pass their hands through the outer shell of the aura they are confronted with a feeling much like placing their hands into a thick viscous slime. In order to improve our bodily health and return our energy system back to its original state we need to learn how to clear this negative information from the aura. This will happen naturally to some degree through our internal arts practice but Nei Gong has specific techniques to achieve these aims which we will look at in Chapter 3 (see pages 91–92).

These are the main components of the energy body which we must be aware of at an early stage in our Nei Gong training. Throughout the later chapters of this book we will also introduce other parts of the energy body as they become relevant.

THE CONSCIOUSNESS BODY

The consciousness body is the furthest of the three bodies of man from the physical realm. It vibrates at a similar frequency to the energy of the Dao and connects to our mind through the highly refined energy of Shen. The consciousness body is above the constraints of the three-dimensional realm and so is difficult to explain in an exact manner; instead we have several conceptual frameworks to give us some idea of how our consciousness is constructed. One of these theories is the theory of Heart-Mind which is primarily a Buddhist framework although it has also been adopted by the Daoist traditions. Figure 2.25 shows the conceptual framework of the Heart-Mind.

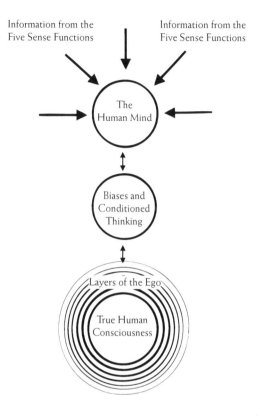

Information from the
Five Sense Functions

Information from the
Five Sense Functions

The
Human Mind

Biases and
Conditioned
Thinking

Layers of the Ego

True Human
Consciousness

Figure 2.25 The Heart-Mind

In Daoist thought, the great power of Dao is permanent along with
the entities of Heaven and Earth. Everything else is transient in nature
as it is subject to the laws of form and so the three-dimensional realm.
The three-dimensional realm is in turn subject to the rules of time,
progress, development and ultimately decline. This is the fate of man
and all matter that exists within our universe. These laws are reflected
within human consciousness and the various layers of transience and
permanence are known collectively as the Heart-Mind.

True consciousness is born directly from Dao through the
'opening' of the mysterious pass. True consciousness has many names
such as 'Buddha nature', 'true nature', 'magical knowing', 'enlightened
wisdom', etc. It is this part of the Heart-Mind which we are trying to

access through our practices and this is what forms the foundation for the creation of the consciousness body. The problem with accessing this part of the consciousness body is that there is a direct relationship taking place between the energy body and the physical body which are transient in nature. Unlike the consciousness body, they will not continue to exist forever and so will at some point break down and cease to exist.

The connecting part of the energy system with the consciousness body is the middle Dan Tien. Here the conversion of Qi to Shen takes place and the manifestation of the five elemental energies of the acquired meridians take shape. It is from this point that we are able to experience the energetic manifestation of the consciousness body as it relates to the 'reality' we live within. These manifestations are our emotions which we have already looked at in this chapter (see pages 51–53).

When our emotions get involved in the thought processes of our consciousness we begin to form a new entity which is usually known within the Western world as our Ego. The Ego is the 'false sense of our self' that we build up in our mind and then allow to govern our thoughts, speech and actions. Like a mask that we all hide behind it prevents us from being honest or spontaneous in anything that we do. The main goal of spiritual traditions like Buddhism and Daoism is the erosion of the Ego, which is preventing us from attaining spiritual elevation.

The layers of the Ego lie on top of our true consciousness like numerous shells which need to be stripped away in our practice so that we may reconnect with the core elements of our Heart-Mind which are usually known as the 'seed consciousness'. This is easier said than done as any serious practitioner of meditation will tell you.

The key to ending the control that the Ego has over us is the development of true internal awareness. If we can reconnect our mind with the vibrational frequency of the consciousness body and balance our connection to the three bodies of man then we will find the mysterious pass. As talked about above; the mysterious pass is the doorway through which enlightenment can come forth as it is the key to dissolving the layers of our Ego.

In some Daoist texts they talk about there being more bodies of man. These number at around eight or sometimes as many as 64. These extra bodies of man are in fact all just layers of the consciousness body.

In my opinion it is too difficult to start trying to work with all of these different layers of reality which exist within our consciousness. It is possible to focus on just the three we talk about here and still get the desired results. Daoist theory can be complex enough already without adding even more information!

COMMUNICATION ACROSS THE THREE ENERGY BODIES OF MAN

We have discussed the various elements of the three bodies of man according to Daoist thought in this chapter. It is advisable that you spend some time going over the information in this section to familiarise yourself with the framework you are working with when practising Nei Gong. You will begin your practice by conditioning the physical body in the correct way, then you will learn how to access the energy body and then finally the consciousness body.

The problem is that each of the three bodies 'speak different languages' and we need to find a translator. Thankfully there are some simple intermediaries we can access through our practice. The first is our breathing which enables us to share information across the physical and energy bodies. We will now look at this in detail within the next chapter when we discuss Sung breathing.

CHAPTER 3

SUNG BREATHING

Breath work is one of the most important parts of the Daoist tradition. It was long ago realised that understanding and working with our breathing was the most effective way to build a bridge between the physical and energetic realms.

Human beings breathe from the second we are born right through to the moment we die. It is the single most repeated action throughout our entire life and yet we tend to do it very badly! Most people take the act of respiration for granted and don't realise that the efficiency of our breathing is closely linked to the health of our mind and body.

There are several different breathing techniques taught within Daoism but easily the most useful method for Nei Gong practice is a type of abdominal breathing known as 'Sung breathing'.

The process of changing the way we work with our breath is as follows:

- First, we consciously take control of our breathing. We need to over-ride the unconscious process which allows us to breathe without thinking.

- Second, we learn how to Sung breathe.

- Then we return control of our breathing to the unconscious processes having retrained our body's natural breathing process to a new, more efficient method.

Sung breathing is a technique which, although simple, has profound effects on health and consciousness. Benefits range from relaxing the body right the way through to helping you reconnect with the two great powers of Heaven and Earth. In this chapter we are going to look closely at the process of Sung breathing and the positive changes it will bring about in your training given enough time.

Basic Purposes of Regulating the Breath

Our breathing serves a multitude of purposes but on a basic level it enables us to carry out the following tasks:

- bring oxygen into the body

- expel carbon dioxide from the body which would otherwise be harmful

- regulate our emotions to a certain extent

- increase our acquired Qi intake

- regulate the internal pressure of the torso

- reconnect to the powers of Heaven and Earth.

The above functions of breathing enable us to develop a strong foundation for further Nei Gong training.

Increasing Oxygen Intake

Oxygen is taken in through our lungs, passed into the blood stream and then in turn reaches every cell, tissue and organ in the body. Oxygen is obviously essential to human existence and so it makes sense for any internal practice that we try to maximise the amount of oxygen we can take in and use.

Our brain cells absorb vast quantities of oxygen and so if we wish to improve and maintain our mental capacity then our breathing must be as efficient as possible. Without this oxygen our mental focus becomes weaker and we cannot concentrate properly. If we wish to maintain our mental faculties into later life then Sung breathing will be of great use to us.

A lot of the early bodywork in Nei Gong relies on being able to softly open up and stretch the body. In order for muscles to relax and lengthen they need to be oxygenated and so we can see that breathing and flexibility are closely linked.

Increasing the Rate of Carbon Dioxide Expulsion

If there is an excess of carbon dioxide within the body, our breathing will speed up in order to expel this toxic waste product from our blood stream. This will result in shallow breathing high in the chest. This is counter-productive since it means that some carbon dioxide will remain within the lower parts of the lungs for much longer. It is far better to train the breath to be smoother and longer so that the entire lung is used and cleaned out.

An excess of carbon dioxide will mean that less oxygen is absorbed as we breathe and so we will experience diminished brain function and stamina levels. Over time excess carbon dioxide can lead to illness.

Regulating our Emotions

In Chapter 2 we looked at how the emotions are nothing more than an energetic manifestation of the state of our consciousness body. The framework we use to understand this is the Heart-Mind theory.

Our breathing alone does not allow us to access the consciousness body directly but it does allow us to calm the emotions and regulate them to some degree. Whilst this is not a permanent way to attain stillness within the centre of our mind it is enough to give us a glimpse of this level of clarity which is required for the intermediate and higher levels of Nei Gong.

Our breathing and our emotions are linked as shown in Figure 3.1.

May serve to calm or stress the emotions

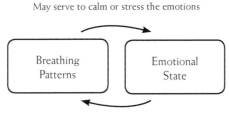

Can cause the breathing to become shallow or deep

Figure 3.1 The Respiration and Emotional Cycle

It is easy to see how people experience shifts in the breathing patterns when they are experiencing strong emotions. Anger often produces short, rasping breaths high in the chest. Sadness makes people draw in long sighing breaths as though the body is struggling to get air.

It is important to understand that if our emotions affect our breathing, our breathing can affect our emotions. The transient emotions lie on top of our true nature like a stormy sea which is always in turmoil. Through regulation of our breathing the sea can be calmed and made still.

Increasing our Acquired Qi Intake

Qi can be divided into several different categories. Acquired Qi is the energy we take into our body from the environment after we are born. This energy is taken mainly from our food and air; it is mixed within the body. As well as oxygen, our breathing enables us to draw in the Qi from our environment and we obviously wish to maximise this if we are to get the most from our Nei Gong training.

Regulating the Internal Pressure of the Torso

Our torso is divided into two main chambers by the diaphragm, the thoracic cavity and abdominal cavity. This is shown in Figure 3.2.

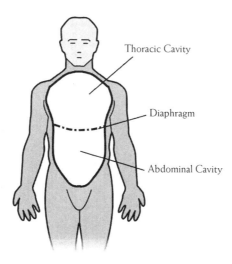

Thoracic Cavity

Diaphragm

Abdominal Cavity

Figure 3.2 The Cavities of the Human Torso and the Diaphragm

Breathing causes the diaphragm to move up and down which alternates the physical and energetic pressure of the two cavities.

'Like bellows, Dao breathes between Heaven and Earth,

Empty, yet potent,

Its motive force generates the myriad things.'

The alternating internal pressure of the moving diaphragm through our breathing helps us to become these bellows which exist between the realms of Heaven and Earth. We will look at this in further detail towards the end of this chapter as this concept is the key to getting the most from Sung breathing (see pages 93–99).

Even before we reach this stage of acting as an 'internal bellows' there are more physical benefits to be had from moving the diaphragm efficiently. The alternating air pressure within the thoracic and abdominal cavities causes the organs to be gently squeezed and released as you breathe. This serves as an internal massage which helps to maintain the longevity of the organs. It is for this reason that we must be careful not to breathe too forcefully. Too much pressure is detrimental to the organs; in particular the kidneys and the digestive system are prone to damage from forceful breathing. Everything we do within Daoist Nei Gong should feel like a naturally evolving unforced process.

Reconnecting to the Powers of Heaven and Earth

At the highest stage of Sung breathing we are able to empty out the body and reconnect to the two great vibrational powers which, according to Daoist philosophy, gave birth to life. Sung breathing is the key to developing energetic root which is our link to the Earth and energetic emptiness which is the key to reconnecting to the energy of Heaven.

If we can do this then we have attained a high level of skill in the internal arts.

THE PRINCIPLE OF SUNG

It is not enough to simply relax during practice of Nei Gong or indeed any of the internal arts. The Daoists use the term 'Sung' instead of 'relax' for good reason. In brief, Sung can be translated as: the systematic transference of habitual tension from either the physical or consciousness body into the energetic realm.

This may sound a little confusing but in essence it is quite simple as long as we remember that Sung is an energetic process which largely takes place within the energy body.

Figure 3.3 shows how the theory of Sung is applied to the three bodies of man.

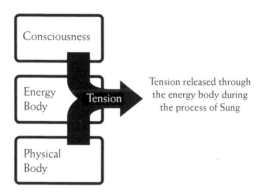

Figure 3.3 The Process of Sung

The key to transforming physical tension and tension from the consciousness body into energetic factors which can be released is to develop harmonisation of the three bodies of man through our breathing.

Tension within the physical body is simply a piece of information which is stored as a vibration. This tension may have been caused by any number of physical or emotional factors which, for the most part, we will be unaware of during the process of Sung. As we use our Sung breathing technique, the frequency of this vibration alters. It is transformed into an energetic state and so moved into the meridian system before being discharged from the body. The result is that our physical tension fades away. The more we practise this process, the deeper we can delve and so we find that tension which has been stored deep within us is released leaving us feeling lighter and more mobile. Many of my students have expressed a great sense of 'relief' after practising even the earliest stages of Sung breathing in my classes.

The process of ridding the body of physical tension is a long and difficult process that moves through the following stages:

- removal of tension from the large muscle groups

- removal of tension from the semi-fluid connective tissues such as ligaments, tendons and most importantly fascia

- removal of tension from the deeper layers of fascia which sit deep within the body, particularly the layers surrounding the organs.

As the deepening layers of physical tension begin to vanish you will notice different changes taking place within your body. Your posture will begin to change as the bones are allowed to 'relax' back into their natural position. The tension which pulled them out of place is let go of and so you should immediately start to notice aches and pains disappearing. You will find that your flexibility increases as joints loosen and the spaces between your bones open up. As the ever-deepening layers of fascia loosen, internal movement will increase and your entire body will soften; the feeling is much like the body of a small child which is very pliable and rubbery.

One of the major changes that you will find is an increase in your stamina levels. It is very draining for the body to store tension and letting go of it means that you will feel refreshed and full of 'zest'.

TENSION WITHIN THE ENERGETIC BODY

The energetic body will store tension as blockages in the various pathways of the meridian system. It is impossible for physical imbalance not to be reflected in an energetic imbalance. These blockages within the meridian system decrease the efficiency of Qi flow and so in turn can lead to sickness.

Qi is driven through the meridian system by the rotation of the lower Dan Tien (described in Chapter 2). The nature of this Qi is constantly changing in response to various factors including our health, emotional state and the quality of the Qi which we draw in from our food and air. The energy body is capable of naturally expelling a certain amount of energetic imbalances when we breathe but, due to the nature of modern living, we tend to develop more imbalances than we can effectively deal with in this way. Through learning the Sung breathing technique we clear tensions or blockages in the meridian system far more effectively. They are mainly expelled through our extremities and several major energy points including:

Laogong (PC8), Yongquan (K1) and Baihui (GV20), provided that they are effectively opened through our internal training.

TENSION WITHIN THE CONSCIOUSNESS BODY

Tension within the consciousness body is manifested as imbalances within our psychological state of being. In the same way that the physical body can develop tensions through injury and illness, the consciousness body can build up tension through the various stresses and difficulties we face in our daily lives. As soon as we have an awareness of the negativity within life we are developing tension within the consciousness body. From a young age we are damaging our psychological state and building up layers of emotional debris. These can manifest in later life as some sort of physical illness or an emotional breakdown.

Our emotions are simply a manifestation of imbalances within the consciousness body. That is not to say that we are trying to rid ourselves of our emotions through our practice, instead we are trying to bring them to a stable point rather than experiencing constant emotional fluctuations which is the case for the vast majority of people.

Sung breathing uses the method of transforming consciousness tension into energetic tension so that it can be removed from the body. Consciousness tension is converted down from the frequency of Shen to Qi whilst physical tension is converted up from the frequency of Jing to Qi. In this way we are finding the 'middle path' in our practice. This is a common aim in both Daoist and Buddhist practices. It is important to note that the later stages of Nei Gong training are more akin to meditative and alchemical practices and so consciousness body tension is simply removed directly via the mind. It does not pass down into the energy body first. Sung breathing is not as advanced as this and could be considered an intermediate practice which helps provide the foundation for further development into meditation. For this stage in our Nei Gong training it is more than adequate and one advantage that it has over meditation is that it does not rely on us being able to achieve the difficult stillness of the mind.

THE TENSION CYCLE

It is important to note that the removal of tension through Sung breathing is not a linear process. When you initially begin it will feel as though you are only working on a physical level but this is not true. Your mind is only capable of tuning in to the physical body and so you will be unaware of the process of Sung affecting you on any other level even though it is taking place. As you practise more you will discover that you are able to feel the various changes taking place on different levels and this will help to train your mind in tuning in to the energy and consciousness body.

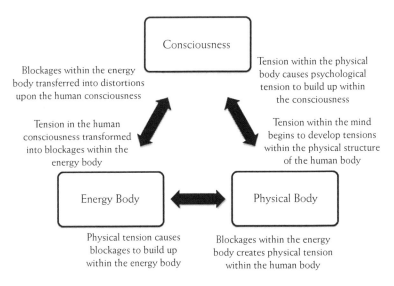

Figure 3.4 The Tension Cycle

Figure 3.4 shows the cycle of tension, which we know as the mind-body connection in Western thought. It shows how there cannot be tension in any one of the three bodies without the other two being affected; this is due to the transference of information which is constantly taking place between the three substances of Jing, Qi and Shen within the human body.

It is important to remember that you will pick up tension through your life and so it is impossible to simply let go of all the tension stored within you and then remain in this state. The process of Sung is ongoing and must take place throughout all of your training if you are to ever reach a high level in any of the internal arts. This is the main reason for retraining your natural breathing process to match the methodology of Sung breathing.

STAGES OF SUNG BREATHING

Although sung breathing is not traditionally broken down into stages, I have found that teaching systematic stages is useful for students enabling them to get a better grasp of how it works. For this reason I present Sung breathing in the following manner:

Stage 1

- Breathe in Tranquillity
- Breathe out Tension

Stage 2

- Breathing with Heaven and Earth

Both stages have their associated exercise that will enable you to get a feel of the progress you are making. Stage 1 deals mainly with the various layers of tension we have already been discussing. Stage 2 leads us into the deeper aspects of Daoist breathing exercises.

BEGINNING SUNG BREATHING

Before we can start to move through the two stages of Sung breathing, we need to develop an awareness of the physical act of breathing. We need to become acquainted with the various movements taking place within our torso. This may sound easy but it can take some time to develop even this level of internal sensitivity.

It is best to carry out the following practice early in the day when you first rise or in the evening prior to sleep provided that you are not too tired. If you practise at these times then it is easier to keep the concerns of the rest of the day out of your mind. Find a peaceful place where you will not be disturbed and begin with around 10 to 15 minutes of practice; you will probably find that this time will naturally begin to expand to up to an hour's practice every day as you relax into the exercise.

The exercise is best practised in either of the two positions shown in Figure 3.5.

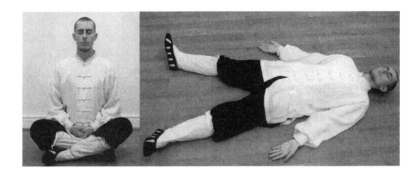

Figure 3.5 Sung Practice Positions

In either of these two positions you are going to practise linking your mind to your breathing. Gently close your eyes and mouth, touch your tongue to the roof of your mouth and breathe in and out through your nose as this helps to warm and filter the air as it enters your body.

Try to forget everything except for your practice. Just allow the mind to relax and empty of all thoughts. At first this will be difficult and the mind will start to produce a veritable medley of images and concerns as it is left to its own devices. Don't try to stop this, just allow the mind to run through these thoughts and eventually find its own natural state of quiet. If you try to force your mind to quiet then you will create more tensions within the consciousness which are counter-productive to your practice.

Once your mind has begun to quieten you are ready to begin following your breath. It is unlikely that you will manage to totally silence the mind of thoughts at this stage so instead wait until it has quietened enough that you are able to focus on what is happening inside your body. Work through the following process:

- Follow the movement of air as it enters your nose.

- Follow the movement of air down into your lungs.

- Feel as your lungs fill with air and the diaphragm moves downwards into the abdominal cavity.

- Feel as the lungs empty and air begins to move back out of the nose.

- Repeat this process and keep observing the above processes taking place.

It is important that you do not use a strong focus. Too much focus at this stage can actually cause Qi to stagnate and your breathing to become forced. You should have the feeling of being a passive observer to the process taking place before you; your mind should be following, not leading.

Your breathing will begin to slow down and move to lower parts of the lungs. Many people are surprised at how they are using their upper chest to breathe and how much calmer they feel straight away when they begin this practice. There are numerous benefits to your physical and emotional health to be had from this practice alone. It is best to build a strong foundation at this stage in your Sung breathing practice before you move on. Spend some months simply practising this exercise so that it begins to feel more natural; it will not be long before your natural breathing process begins to change for the better.

STAGE 1 OF SUNG BREATHING: BREATHE IN TRANQUILLITY AND BREATHE OUT TENSION

Now you are ready to begin releasing tension from the physical, energetic and consciousness bodies using the principle of Sung. You will have built up a strong foundation from the previous exercise and have probably already noticed some changes to your health and state of mind.

Breathing in tranquillity is an important concept and one that can benefit many people straightaway. In order to get the most from our Nei Gong training and indeed the rest of our lives we need to find a way to be at peace. Many people have difficulty bringing their mind into a calm state when in fact the easiest way is to use your breathing. There is great joy and contentment to be had from simply breathing in deeply and filling the body with fresh air. Our body is the one thing that accompanies us throughout our lives constantly, it is the only physical entity which truly belongs to us and it is of utmost importance that we look after it. A great deal of mental stress and discomfort can come from being 'uncomfortable' within your own body and carrying unnecessary tensions.

Try this simple exercise. Next time you feel stressed in any way then use it as a way to see if you have attained the skill of breathing in tranquillity. Take several deep breaths through your nose and allow your lungs to fill with air. Let your mind trace the movement of air down into your lungs as before and then try to take your attention further. Instead of simply being aware of how the lungs and body move, start to develop an awareness of how your body function is altered. It will not be long before you notice how the increased intake of oxygen nourishes the tissues and organs, how your mind feels 'fresher' and there is a general feeling of invigoration. If you can achieve this simple skill then you have managed to breathe in tranquillity.

Breathing out tension is the next stage in your practice. It is best to start with working on your physical tension as this is the easiest layer of imbalance for the majority of people to feel.

As you are practising breathing, allow your mind to gently move over the surface of your body looking for any feelings of discomfort or pain. Due to your body relaxing a little from the Sung breathing and your awareness being traced over your body you will find that many spots of discomfort appear. You will no doubt find many areas of tightness that have gone undetected up until now and even old pains that came from injuries you had forgotten about.

A good area to start with is the chest and torso as releasing physical tension here will allow the lungs to open up and improve your breathing practice. Pay special attention to the inter-costal muscles between the ribs and the area around the diaphragm. If there is tension here then your breathing is still being restricted.

To begin releasing tension, allow your focus to gently hover over the area of discomfort whilst you continue breathing. There is no need for any form of visualisation or mental intervention whilst the process of releasing tension is taking place. Simply continue to breathe and casually observe as each exhalation allows the discomfort to fade away. Some pains will go almost immediately whilst others will take some time and you will probably have to return to them many times until they are gone.

You may assist in the removal of the tension by making very small muscular movements as you gently focus on the tension. These movements should be so small that to an outside observer they are almost invisible.

The key to successfully breathing out your tension is not to get frustrated. This exercise can take some time to get through. Just as you think you have managed to release all of your tension, another layer appears. Like peeling away the layers of an onion you should begin to move deeper and deeper into your body where habitual tension will be stored.

Be sure to work over your entire body. To assist with this process I suggest you try to work through the following areas of your body; if you try to stick to this sequence each time you practise your Sung breathing it will ensure that you do not miss any major areas of your body.

- The chest, diaphragm and inter-costal muscles.

- The shoulders and neck.

- The length of the spine and inter-vertebral spaces.

- The buttocks.

- The hips and groin.

- The knees, ankles and metatarsal spaces of the foot.

- Biceps, triceps, elbows, wrists and fingers.

- The Atlas bone at the base of the skull.

- The face, eye sockets and jaw.

- The last stage is to go deeper into the body and work on any physical tension which sits in the fascia around your organs and tissues. This level of internal sensitivity will take some time to develop but it will appear naturally in time.

Releasing Energetic Tension

After some time your mind will naturally begin to tune in to the frequency of the energy body. This will be a natural development which you do not need to force. When the mind is ready, it will begin to feel the various movements of Qi taking place within your body.

By the time you reach this stage of internal awareness, you will already have been working on releasing tensions or blockages through your Sung breathing practice.

There are several signs to look for:

- First, you will notice a deep heat moving through your body as you breathe. This will reach the temperature of a warm bath or perhaps more. This is actually the increased movement of blood within the body which is being stimulated by Qi movement.

- As you manage to feel movement within the meridians which run near the surface of your body you are likely to feel a tingling or tickling sensation which is much like insects running over you. This is Qi flowing within the acquired meridians.

- The movement of Qi in your Etheric body or aura is an interesting sensation which tends to develop next. As you exhale, your aura will expand away from you and as you inhale it will move in towards the centre of your body. It produces a very relaxing feeling which is much like the tide washing over your body in time with your breathing.

- Movement within the deeper congenital meridians is an interesting stage of internal development. Qi moves through us as a vibrational wave. This wave contains information and each person's mind can interpret the information in a different way. I have come across many different sensations including the feeling of being wet inside as though water is flowing strongly around your body, cold moving through you, intense warmth that pulses and spirals. All of these sensations are normal and nothing to be concerned about. It is easy for us to attach the concepts of good and bad to these sensations but it is counter-productive to our practice.

Enjoy the various sensations that come with your energetic awareness. As before, allow your mind to casually observe what is happening and follow the various movements of Qi taking place. Over time the feelings will become far more tangible sensations.

'Sometimes his breathing is powerful,

Sometimes it is natural,

Sometimes he creates expansion,

Sometimes he simply succumbs,

Avoid excess.'

It is particularly useful at this point to begin following the movements of your aura as it moves in and out with the breath. Follow this movement for some time until you have a strong awareness of the Qi field permeating your skin on each inhalation and expanding out into your surroundings as you exhale (Figure 3.6). It will not be long before you find that you have managed to develop an awareness of the space around you, your sense of feeling is no longer restricted to the limits of your physical body. If you can achieve this ability to a high degree then you are doing very well with your Sung breathing.

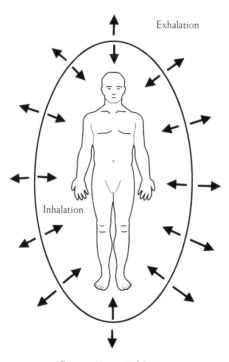

Exhalation

Inhalation

Figure 3.6 Movement of the Aura

The various elements of your energy body form a complex network which would be far too complex to try to release tensions from directly. Getting your mind to work through each and every branch of the meridian system could easily take several lifetimes but thankfully we have a simpler method.

Once you have developed a strong feeling of the movement of your aura you can begin to influence its movements. As you exhale, begin to gradually increase the strength of your intention.[1] Rather than being a casual observer as you have been until this point, use your intention to expand your aura on each exhalation. Gradually inflate the limits of your energetic field as if you are inflating a balloon. Continue until it has expanded several meters from you. The exact size of your aura will vary and it will take some trial and error to discover the exact limits you can reach. If you try to push too far it will be as though your balloon has burst and you will have to start again.

Once the aura has reached its limit simply allow your intention to rest here and the process of releasing tension from your energy body will take place on its own.

Sensations During Energetic Release

As energetic tension is released you are likely to have one or more of the following physical sensations which are a natural sign that your practice is progressing well:

- A stronger sense of tingling or heat as Qi and blood flow increase and move out of your body.

- A cold wind may begin blowing through and out of your body as though you have developed a puncture. This is a good sign that Qi is moving effectively and that blockages are clearing.

- You may lose feeling of your physical body as your mind has attuned completely to the movements of your energetic body. This is a positive happening as it allows your energetic body to begin reconfiguring itself through your Sung practice.

- Deeply rooted energetic blockages may suddenly manifest as discomfort which feels like a deep bruise. This will be uncomfortable but will pass as you continue this practice. Simply keep your intention on your energetic field and allow the discomfort to move out of your body and fade away.

---

1 With regard to Nei Gong practice, intention is different from your awareness. When using your awareness you are allowing your mental focus to follow a process which is already taking place. When using your intention you have a slightly more assertive mindset and aim to use your mind to begin a process. In this particular case you are aiming to lead the movement of your Qi.

- Strong energetic movements may manifest as physical movements. This can come as a surprise at first but is nothing to worry about. Your body may begin to vibrate or shake as the Qi is released. Perhaps your limbs will twitch or spasm for a period of time.

Continue with this practice and simply allow all of these happenings to take place. We have already seen that the energetic and physical bodies are intertwined and so releases from one will affect the other. After you have finished your practice look for changes in your health and well-being. Do not be surprised if for a short while afterwards you feel a little drained or like you are coming down with a cold. These are symptoms of negative Qi leaving the body and similar to what therapists call a 'healing crisis'. These negative feelings will not last long and are actually a positive sign that your training is progressing in the right direction.

Releasing Tension from the Consciousness Body

It is difficult to tune directly into the movements of the consciousness body through Sung breathing alone. A lot of work with the nature of your consciousness must be carried out within the higher stages of Nei Gong training and meditation. For now it is enough to look at the surface layer of the consciousness: the emotions.

According to Daoist thought your emotions are simply energetic movements that take place within your body. They are transient in nature and so constantly swinging your mind from one extreme to the other. Through our practice we are trying to release any excessive emotional energy which will enable us to find a more balanced psychological state.

We will look at the nature of the emotions in more detail later in the book but for now it is enough to have a basic knowledge of the five main energetic movements which characterise our emotions. The five movements are linked in to the five elements of Fire, Metal, Water, Wood and Earth as shown in Table 3.1.

Table 3.1 Emotions and their Energetic Movements

Emotion	Energetic Movement	Element
Excitation	Expansion	Fire
Worry	Division	Earth
Sadness	Contraction	Metal
Fear	Sinking	Water
Anger	Shooting out	Wood

The five movements of energy outlined above are constantly taking place within the body in a cycle. When the emotions are balanced then this cycle continues in a positive manner and is known as the 'construction' cycle. If one of these emotions then moves out of balance then the relationship of the five elements is affected and this can lead to imbalance.

When we wish to release an emotion we don't begin searching for them within ourselves. We just allow them to appear of their own accord whilst we are expanding to clear energy body tensions. They can be experienced as one of two things. First, they may appear as a direct experience of one of the emotions. You may suddenly feel a little sad, scared, angry, excited, etc., during your training. If this happens don't worry. Just acknowledge the emotional switch as an energetic movement and allow it to pass and clear through your expansion. The emotion should not last more than a minute or so. If it does then don't panic and don't attach yourself to the emotional experience taking place. Don't make your emotional imbalances who you are. Just stop the exercise, slowly stand and walk around for a short time until the emotion passes before you return to your practice. The second way you can experience the emotion is as one of the five energetic movements outlined in Table 3.1. For example, an old feeling of sadness may manifest as a feeling of your Qi shrinking in towards your centre. An old feeling of anger might feel like a sudden rush of energy moving from one point in the body to another. Simply allow this to happen and do not analyse it too deeply.

When you have begun to experience these releases taking place you should notice a big difference in your psychological state. This change should slowly become more permanent until it begins to permeate into every facet of your life.

STAGE 2 OF SUNG BREATHING: BREATHE WITH HEAVEN AND EARTH

This next stage in Sung breathing practice is an advanced Daoist teaching which has not been widely passed on in the West. It is applicable to all of the internal arts but can only be achieved to any real degree if a strong foundation has been built in the previous exercises outlined here.

A key concern to the ancient Daoists was learning to live in unison with the two great powers of Heaven and Earth. It was stated within the *Dao De Jing* that:

'Humanity follows the Earth,

Earth follows Heaven,

Heaven follows Dao,

Dao follows the principle of Ziran.'

This line from the *Dao De Jing* shows us the order by which we need to connect to the energies which surround us. If we follow this route then we will be led back to Dao (the Way) which is the goal of Daoist practices.

The second stage of Sung breathing practice begins to reconnect us first to Earth by helping us develop an energetic route. Further practice will enable us to empty out the energy body and so reconnect with the power of Heaven.

Reconnecting to Earth

Like human beings, the Earth has its own energy system which runs across its surface and deep within its centre. The core of the planet rotates like our lower Dan Tien and this helps to direct vibrational frequencies throughout its various energetic pathways. If we can drop an energetic root down into the planet then we are able to draw upon the energy of the Earth and so use it to further our training.

The key to developing an energetic root is to understand the relationship between the cycle of Sung breathing and the movement of energetic pressure in the abdominal cavity. To help develop a feeling for this exercise we are going to practise a second breathing method.

Figure 3.7 Standing for Sung Practice

As we inhale, our diaphragm descends into the abdomen which causes our belly to expand. The expansion of our belly is due to an increase of pressure in the abdominal cavity. As well as this physical pressure there is also an energetic pressure which usually assists in the movement of Qi across the upper and lower parts of the body. To develop an awareness of this pressure we are going to hold our breath after the inhalation.

Practise this exercise in a neutral standing position as shown in Figure 3.7. Ensure that all of your alignments are correct and that you have rid your body of as many tensions as possible. This exercise is difficult to practise lying down at first.

Inhale as before and fill the lungs with air. This time keep your awareness within your abdominal cavity and then hold your breath. Do not over-strain your body by holding your breath for too long a period of time; a few seconds is enough. Next exhale as before with your mind still in the abdominal cavity and then do the same again; hold your breath for a few seconds before you inhale.

Carry on like this for some time until you are comfortable with the rhythm of this exercise. At first it might create some physical tension; if this happens, return to the previous stage of releasing tension until it fades away.

Now pay attention to the nature of the energy within your abdominal cavity when you are holding your breath at the end of the inhalation. If you have managed to develop a good level of awareness of your energy body then you will be able to feel that there is an increase in Qi in this area of the body at this time. It will vibrate at a higher frequency and feel as though it is trying to escape. This is the increased energetic pressure which is natural when you breathe in. Depending upon how open the meridians in your lower body are, this Qi will do one of two things when you exhale:

- If your meridians are still full of numerous blockages then only a small amount of it will move down into the legs. The majority of it will disperse or move back into various parts of your body where it will circulate within the meridians system again.

- If your legs have been sufficiently aligned, softened and the meridians within your lower body have been cleared sufficiently then this Qi will move in a strong wave down through your legs into the feet. Holding your breath momentarily and focusing upon the increase in internal pressure amplifies this feeling so that you will gain a strong awareness of this Qi movement.

If the Qi is effectively moving down your legs it is likely that you will at first feel a physical movement that goes along with your energetic root developing. Your legs will feel as if they are collapsing and you are being drawn down to the floor. You will probably feel very heavy and it is not uncommon for people to be pulled to the floor on their knees or face. Sometimes the energetic pull of the root is so strong that people are held fast to the floor for some time. Do not worry if this happens; just allow it to take place. It is a temporary stage of development and after a while you will be able to remain standing whilst the Qi drops down through your legs.

As the Qi hits your feet it will begin to open up one of the major energy gates of your body which is situated on the base of your feet. This point is known as Yongquan (K1) and is shown in Figure 3.8.

As this point opens you will notice an increase in heat in the base of your feet. The heat may sometimes get so hot that I have had students describe their feet feeling as though they are burning! Do not worry though, it will do you no harm and when the feeling has passed, you will have opened Yongquan. Qi will now be able to move down out of your feet into the floor and develop an internal root which connects you to the planet. It is interesting to note that as this point opens, the bones of your feet spread apart and many

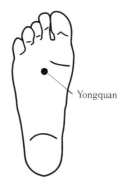

Yongquan

Figure 3.8 Yongquan

people find that they have gone up a shoe size doing this exercise. Once you have this root you will find that you feel a great deal more stable and that your balance has drastically improved. Practitioners of the art of Taiji will find that this root helps to improve their pushing hands.

Now we need to focus on what is taking place when we hold our breath at the end of the exhalation. Drop your focus down to the base of your feet and your legs. After some time you will find that a vibration begins to appear in your legs. This vibration is coiled around your bones and rises up into the Kua and lower abdomen as shown in Figure 3.9.

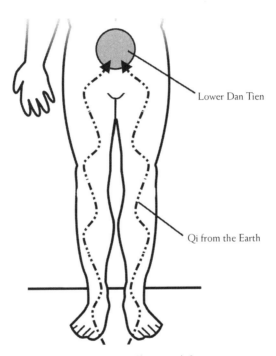

Lower Dan Tien

Qi from the Earth

Figure 3.9 Vibrations in the Legs

As you begin to inhale a movement of Qi begins to take place from the floor to the Kua. It travels up through the Yongquan point, around the lines of vibration you could feel and up into the abdomen. This movement of Qi is the energy of the Earth being drawn into your body. Just like in the last stage, there are often some spontaneous physical movements to experience when this stage of internal development is taking place. As the planet's Qi moves up into your body you will find that you are completely uprooted and thrown up into the air. This is a temporary stage that will not last long, do not worry if it happens; instead enjoy the strange sensation of the planet making you jump around comically!

If you can achieve both of these and the spontaneous physical movements have gone then you are ready to begin integrating this process into your regular Sung breathing.

Begin to slowly decrease the time that you spend holding your breath. Do this gradually to ensure that you can still drop your root and draw up earth-force. If you lose the feeling then progress more slowly. After some practice you should be able to return to breathing normally without holding your breath at all. If you can do this then you have successfully integrated earth-force connection into your subconscious breathing patterns.

The Advantage of Connecting to the Earth

The Qi of the planet vibrates at the same frequency as your Jing, the base element from which all physical creation is born. As the Qi of the Earth moves into the body it is led up to the kidney area of the body and in particular a point known as Mingmen. This helps to nourish the body's essence which dictates various aspects of your health as well as the speed at which your body ages. Drawing in the planet's Qi is one of the main Daoist practices which leads to longevity.

The planet's Qi also has a cleansing effect on the entire meridian system and can help to keep Qi stagnation and blockages to a minimum. This helps to lay the foundation for the next stage which is connection to Heaven through Sung Breathing.

Connecting to Heaven

The next stage in Sung breathing is learning to reconnect to the energy of Heaven. When Daoists talk about Heaven they are referring to the various energetic frequencies which surround us in the environment. This is different from Qi contained in the air we breathe; Heaven energy is a more refined frequency than 'air Qi'. It is more akin to the energy of the consciousness body than the Qi of our energy body. In Daoist thought it is Heaven energy (pure Yang) and Earth energy (pure Yin) combining which creates the potential for existence as shown in Figure 3.10.

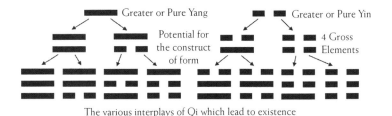

The various interplays of Qi which lead to existence

Figure 3.10 Mixing of Taiyang and Taiyin Qi

If you can develop a strong connection with the Earth then developing a connection to Heaven should be a naturally unfolding process. There is no specific method to attaining this stage. Instead you should continue with your Sung breathing practice as a stand-alone exercise as well as putting it into the rest of your Nei Gong training.

It will take some time before the Earth's Qi integrates itself into your whole energetic system. This relies on awakening the dormant lower Dan Tien as described in Chapter 6. This rotating sphere of energy helps to drive the Qi through the meridians and this in turn awakens further parts of the energy body and mind.

When Heaven Qi moves into your body you will experience the following sensations:

- There will be a stage when your palms begin to heat up in the same way as Yongquan did. This is different from the heat often experienced early on in conventional Qi Gong practice. The heat you experience now is far greater; it is akin to placing your hand on the side of a kettle although strangely it will not burn you. This is the Laogong (PC8) point opening which is another major energy gate of the body.

- You will also experience this heat opening up the Baihui (GV20) point on top of your head. This is a major point for Heaven Qi to flow into the body.

- As Heaven Qi flows into the body, you will have periods of time where you completely lose all sensation of your physical body. This can be slightly unnerving at first but is nothing to worry about; it is a positive stage in your development;

once you relax into them you can enjoy the feeling of being incredibly light and ethereal. This is likely to be the first time that you feel how uncomfortable your physical body really is.

As Heaven Qi filters into your system you will find that your mind becomes increasingly calm and still. It will be much easier to find mental silence during meditative practices and there will be less mental turmoil during your daily life.

This is as far as Sung breathing practice alone can take you. These stages have helped to build a strong foundation within the energetic realm for further training in Nei Gong. Be aware that accomplishing these goals can take a long time and that perseverance is the key here. Do not be disheartened or frustrated and you will surely find the path to the Dao.

'Dissolving his separation,

The sage draws in Heaven and Earth,

And pulses with the cosmos,

Achieving transcendent comprehension,

The true aim of all sages.'

CHAPTER 4

THE JI BEN QI GONG

By now you should have a fairly good idea of what Nei Gong is and how it relates to the philosophy of Daoism. We have also looked at the various elements of the human energy system and the main breathing methodology used when practising Nei Gong. This knowledge provides the foundation for any internal training and you should familiarise yourself with this information. According to Chinese thought: theory is the root of practice.

In this chapter we will look at a simple set of Qi Gong exercises which can be used to practise the principles contained within this book. There are countless different Qi Gong systems being practised around the planet; they vary greatly in nature. Some are very dynamic with complex acrobatic movements whilst others are at the opposite end of the scale with no external movements whatsoever. Each traditional system of Qi Gong was developed to serve a particular purpose. Most were created to improve the practitioner's health but other systems serve to develop internal force for fighting or to open up areas of the mind to assist in meditation. Most systems can be practised together without there being any danger to the practitioner's health but very occasionally there are some exercises which can work against each other. In the majority of cases this will just result in a person's Qi Gong practice being weakened but in some instances it can actually be damaging to a person's health.

The set of eight exercises presented here are known as the 'Ji Ben Qi Gong', which translates as meaning 'fundamental energy exercises'. They are based around the principle of moving the body's joints in the most natural and efficient way possible. They only circulate Qi in the direction which is normal for the meridian system and so they should not clash with any other Qi Gong system. People reading this book who wish to start practising the Nei Gong principles outlined can use these exercises without fear of problems arising in their practice. Due to their simple and efficient nature you can also practise them without it being detrimental to any other regular Qi Gong training regime you may have.

The eight exercises of the Ji Ben Qi Gong are as follows:

- Compressing the Pearl
- Flying Hands
- Opening the Chest
- Upholding the Moon
- Swimming Dragon
- Diagonal Flying
- Cow Turns its Head
- The Heavenly Bow

For each exercise there are instructions on how to carry out the movement along with a little information on their medical function. I do not go into greater depth with regards to their health benefits as I only mean you to have them as a set of tools to practise Nei Gong. Remember that those wishing to practise the more advanced aspects of the internal arts should not see Qi Gong exercises as an end result in their own right. They are simply tools to help you move through the various stages of internal change we know as Nei Gong.

PREPARING FOR JI BEN QI GONG PRACTICE

Begin by lightly clasping your hands over the lower Dan Tien and standing with your feet a shoulder width apart. Suspend the head and open the spine, ensure that you have no unnecessary tension in your body but at the same time do not allow your spine to 'slump' as this will reduce Qi flow within the torso.

Breathe deep into the lower abdomen and allow your mind to gently settle into the lower Dan Tien area. Empty your mind and forget all outside distractions. Remain in this state for a few minutes so that your subconscious may begin to take over the running of your energy system.

EXERCISE 1: COMPRESSING THE PEARL

Figure 4.1 Compressing the Pearl

Slowly allow your hands to drop down to your sides, let all of the tension stored in your upper body and shoulders drain down through the arms and out through the finger tips.

Keeping your hips level; drop your weight a little into your legs and step lightly out to shoulder width with your feet. Maintain your upright but relaxed posture as your attention shifts from the lower Dan Tien to the entire physical body. With a soft focus, be aware of the edge of your physical structure at the same time as observing the inside of your body with your mind. Try to keep the mind empty of outside thoughts as much as possible. You are now ready to perform the first exercise which is known as 'compressing the pearl'.

Lift your hands up to the level of your lower Dan Tien; hold them here for a few breaths. Be aware of the space between your palms at the same time as keeping your focus on your physical and internal structure. The space between your hands is not an exact science but it is roughly the size of a basketball. Make sure that the hands are not tensely forced open but at the same time they should not be limp or closed. The feeling is like lightly stretching the tendons across the palm so that the bones can open up, a little like stretching elastic until it is only just held taut rather than stretched out to its limit.

Gradually inhale as you lift your arms up as shown in Figure 4.1. Do not raise the shoulders to lift your arms, instead try to open the joints in your shoulders, elbows and wrists at the same time to create 'space' in the joints. Your arms should rise until they are almost horizontal from the line of your shoulders. Ensure that you do not lift them too high or you will close off two main energetic pathways within the side channels of your meridian system.

From here, begin to exhale and bring the hands back to their original position in front of the lower Dan Tien.

Use gentle intention as you bring the hands towards each other so that they 'squeeze' the space between the palms. Ensure that this does not create tension within your upper body as the muscles should not engage to create the squeeze.

Repeat this exercise at least eight times (although you should not worry too much about the number of repetitions when you train). What is important is the flow and level of technical detail you manage to maintain throughout the movements.

'Compressing the Pearl' stimulates Qi flow along the Heart, Lung and Pericardium meridians. It is particularly effective at opening the point 'Laogong' (PC8) which is important for internal work.

The movements and internal compressions serve to gently massage the lungs and heart, which in turn improves health and longevity.

After a long period of practice, Qi flow will begin to take place between the lower part of the Triple Heater and the base of the feet to a point known as Yongquan (K1). This is an important point for developing an internal relationship between yourself and the vibrational frequencies of the Earth.

EXERCISE 2: FLYING HANDS

Figure 4.2 Flying Hands

To move on to the second exercise, known as 'Flying Hands', bring your hands in to the lower Dan Tien as in the previous exercise. Now gently begin inhaling as you raise the arms up in front of your body. Allow the hands to naturally turn in towards your body as shown in Figure 4.2.

The lift of your arms is initially driven by the elbows moving upwards but, after time, you will find that the movements naturally begin to be generated by the chest and spine.

Your inhalation should be synchronised with the raising of the arms, which move to the level of your shoulders.

Begin to exhale as the arms unfold in front of you. The feeling is of the arms opening out and away from you.

Using gentle intention, bring the arms down towards the floor as if they are pressing against a large spring in front of you on the ground. Ensure that you do not squeeze your muscles even though the body naturally wants to do so. Any force involved in this exercise should purely be of the internal kind.

Repeat this exercise at least eight times although, again, the exact number is not crucial.

This exercise stimulates internal Qi flow along the Lung, Heart, Pericardium, Large Intestine, Small Intestine and Triple Heater channels. The 'unfolding' movement of the arms assists in drawing stagnant energy away from the diaphragm.

EXERCISE 3: OPENING THE CHEST

Figure 4.3 Opening the Chest

Begin to lift the arms up and out as shown in Figure 4.3. It is important that you do not raise your shoulders, instead initiate the movement by spreading your chest.

Draw the arms up and out in a circular fashion. The rotation of the arms, as they move outwards, should begin at the shoulders. This allows the entire shoulder joint to turn as the chest opens wide and you inhale, filling the lungs with air. It is important to remember that your breathing should be low down in the lungs and the abdomen should expand. It is easy (but incorrect) to slip into 'upper chest' breathing when your arms are lifted in Qi Gong.

This exercise is very expansive. Do not be afraid to really open out the body as wide as possible so that as much oxygen as possible is taken into the body.

As you exhale, allow your arms to naturally move back along the same circular arc back towards the lower Dan Tien area.

This movement is then repeated a minimum of eight times so that your arms move up and out as you inhale and then in and down as you exhale.

The exercise is designed to massage the internal organs of the upper body as well as bring as much oxygen into the blood stream as possible.

The alternating internal pressures generated by this exercise stimulate the lower section of your torso and so massage the digestive system.

EXERCISE 4: UPHOLDING THE MOON

Figure 4.4 Upholding the Moon

This exercise begins from the peak of the inhalation of the previous movement. The arms should be extended away from the body, level with your shoulders and the chest should be open and stretched.

Turn the fingers downwards to face the floor and spend a minute or so standing with your intention gently moving out of the finger tips down towards the floor.

Begin to fold from the 'Kua' (see pages 126–127) and lower the body towards the ground as shown in Figure 4.4. Inhale as you do this.

The spine should be curved just enough so that the posterior spaces between the vertebrae are opened a little. The hands should make a circular, scooping motion so that the outside of the arms are also gently pulled open. Do not squat too low to the ground as this will inhibit energetic flow through the lower body and create tension in the calves.

Unfold the body to stand up. This allows the spine to gently open and stretch upwards. Open the front of your body so that your arms are able to rotate away from you and lift upwards above your head. The palms should now be turning to face upwards and away from you.

Exhale strongly as you push up and away from the body. Do not be conservative with the stretching at this point in the exercise. Use your intention to lead the breath out beyond the arms and hands into the distance on your exhalation.

Continue the exhalation as your arms move down in an arc towards your starting position as shown in Figure 4.4.

Once again, curve the spine a little, stretch across the upper back and lengthen the outside of the arms as you inhale and squat.

Repeat this exercise eight times as before. Ensure that your movements match your breathing.

This exercise stimulates Qi flow across the Bladder, Stomach and Kidney meridians. The spine is opened up which has numerous benefits including increased blood and Qi flow between the upper and lower halves of your body. This exercise also serves to remove any stagnant Qi which may have built up in the Triple Heater during performance of the previous three exercises.

Never under-estimate the importance of stretching and opening the spine during Qi Gong practice.

Exercise 5: Swimming Dragon

Figure 4.5 Swimming Dragon

Begin by standing up from the last exercise and turning your hands to face opposite directions as shown in Figure 4.5. One palm should face the sky whilst the other faces the floor. They should be slightly extended out in front of you with roughly two inches between them. Allow your intention to gently extend from Laogong (PC8) on each palm away from you, one up towards the sky and one down towards the floor.

Exhale as your palms extend away from each other. Ensure that the shoulders are kept level and that you do not tilt your pelvis, which is a common error for beginners. The palms must keep facing the floor and the sky as they move and they must remain on two parallel lines in front of you. Push the arms away from you as far as you can without creating an excess of tension whilst keeping the correct bodily alignments.

Once you have reached the extent of your push, begin to turn the hands over to face the opposite direction, that is to say, if the hand was facing the sky, it now turns to face the floor and vice versa. Breathe in and draw the hands back in to the centre again. You should be back where you began the exercise although you should have your hands the other way around.

Your inhalation ends as the hands draw level with each other.

Now repeat the exercise on the other side of the body. Exhale as you move the hands away from each other again. Repeat the exercises at least eight times to ensure a healthy flow of Qi.

This exercise stimulates Qi flow along the Spleen, Stomach and Liver meridians. It balances the internal energetic pressures of the left and right sides of your torso and strengthens the muscles and ligaments of your torso.

At an advanced level, this exercise can also begin to create a large degree of energetic movement around the girdling meridian, which begins to assist in awakening the lower Dan Tien.

EXERCISE 6: DIAGONAL FLYING

Figure 4.6 Diagonal Flying

Finish the previous exercise by turning the hands to face each other. One palm should be high whilst the other is low as shown in Figure 4.6. It should be almost as if your palms are resting on either side of a sheet of glass. Move your awareness into the space between the palms.

Step a little wider so that you can open your Kua effectively. Ensure that your knees stay in line with your toes. This stance is known as Mabu or 'Horse Riding Stance' in Chinese Gong Fu.

The foot on the same side as your lower palm turns out to 90 degrees as you begin to open your chest in either direction and turn your waist to face the same direction as the foot that just turned.

Exhale as the hands begin to move apart. They travel diagonally in opposite directions with the lead palm facing upwards and the rear hand facing the floor.

The final extension of the posture should put you into the diagonal flying posture. The thumb of the lead hand should face away from you and your mind should extend out into the far distance as you complete your exhalation.

Now begin to inhale and turn your foot back to the front so that you return to Mabu. Your hands move back to the start position although now they should be reversed. The hand that was lower is now higher and vice versa. Your intention should once again squeeze between the palms although the muscles should remain relaxed.

Remain at this point for a few breaths and try to allow any tension to drop down through your hips and legs into the ground. Ensure that although you are relaxing downwards, you keep your spine open and your head suspended. It is important that you do not allow your structure to collapse. If you collapse your structure then your alignments will be thrown out and so you will be reducing Qi flow.

Repeat the exercise on the other side of the body.

Repeat the exercise on each side of your body at least eight times.

This exercise circulates Qi along the Stomach, Spleen, Kidney and Liver meridians.

Advanced practitioners will be able to feel how the exercise enables you to build up and then release internal pressure in the thoracic and abdominal cavities of the torso.

EXERCISE 7: COW TURNS ITS HEAD

Figure 4.7 Cow Turns its Head

Begin this exercise by bringing your feet back in to shoulder width. Make sure that your shoulders and hips stay level as you bring your feet back in towards the centre.

Your arms should settle in front of your chest as if they are holding a large beachball. Let your hands remain level with your chest whilst your elbows hang down as shown in Figure 4.7.

Remain in this position and breathe for a few minutes. You should try to keep your skeletal structure upright and correctly aligned but imagine that all of your muscles and flesh are draining off of you and falling to the floor. Keep this visualisation for some time so that you gradually relax. You will find that your body feels as though it is sinking into the floor even though you are remaining upright.

Turn your body from the 'Kua' to 45 degrees whilst your arms remain in an arc in front of you. Try not to lose the feeling of relaxing into the floor as you turn.

Ensure that you turn around your centre as if you had a pole passing through your body from the perineum to the top of your head. Inhale as you carry out this movement.

Exhale as you extend your hands away from you up at a slight angle into the sky. Part the index fingers and thumbs as the palms turn. Let your gaze settle on the space between your hands and let your intention extend into the distance.

You should try to stretch all of the muscles and ligaments around your torso as you complete this movement. In particular try to open out the ribs and stretch the inter-costal muscles as your hands turn and push away from you. If you remain relaxed enough, you should feel the ligaments pull from your hands, down your arms, through your sides and down into the legs. If you manage this then you have successfully managed to connect the whole body.

As you begin to inhale, return your hands to an arc in front of you and then rotate the body from your Kua to face 45 degrees in the other direction. Repeat the push away from you in the other direction.

Repeat the twist and push in each direction at least eight times to conclude the 'Cow Turns its Head' exercise.

Do not allow the knees to collapse in as you turn your body. Also ensure that a complete circle is maintained between the chest and arms for the duration of this exercise. If an uneven shape is held in the arms then Qi flow is uneven and this may in turn lead to stagnation in the joints of the upper body.

This exercise mainly stimulates Qi flow along the Small Intestine, Triple Heater, Stomach, Spleen, Gallbladder and Liver meridians. The line of intention which you draw as you inhale helps to lead stagnant Qi away from the head and neck. One of the most beneficial aspects of this exercise is that excess heat is drawn away from the heart. This heat, which may otherwise harm the heart, is passed into the lungs and expelled as you exhale.

EXERCISE 8: THE HEAVENLY BOW

The final exercise in the set begins from the circular 'beachball' position of the previous exercise. The only difference is that you should step out back into the wider 'Mabu' stance again as in the 'Diagonal Flying' exercise. Step out slowly and lightly so as not to create any tension in your body.

Figure 4.8 The Heavenly Bow

Remain here in this position for some time and breathe out any tension in the body, which may be created by the wider stance. Use the Sung breathing method to achieve this.

Turn your body 90 degrees to one side from the 'Kua'. Make a shape as if drawing a longbow to your side. The hand which would be drawing the string of the bow forms a loose fist whilst the other hand forms the mudra known as 'secret sword hand' which is shown in Figure 4.9.

The middle and index fingers are almost touching and extended. The thumb is looped over the ring-finger and your 'pinky'. The hand position is designed to circulate Qi around the loop you have formed and then extend the increased flow out of the other fingers. After a while you will be able to feel the

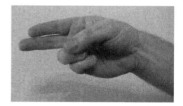

Figure 4.9 Secret Sword Mudra

increased level of heat which can be expelled from the body using this hand position.

Begin to exhale and extend the lead arm away from your body. Point the index and middle fingers into the distance as the rear hand pulls back as if drawing a longbow. Your mind must extend into the distance as the chest is pulled open and your hips twist back to the front. Once the upper body has reached the limit of its extension and you have completed your exhalation, bring the arms back to the original position and relax the body once again.

If you find tension in the body then spend some time in this position using 'Sung breathing' to release any tightness. If you are relaxed and soft then proceed straight into the next repetition.

Carry out the same exercise on the other side of your body. This counts as one time through drawing 'The Heavenly Bow'.

Repeat on each side of the body at least eight times.

This exercise is designed to work directly with the energy of our Kidneys and thus the creation of Zhi or 'will-power'. This is an essential ingredient for our Nei Gong practice, which we will look at in more detail later in the book (see page 194).

The twisting and stretching of the upper body serves to strengthen the muscles and tendons of the upper body whilst the long stance creates a powerful base and strong legs. Stagnant Qi is also driven out of the upper body through the combination of our intention reaching into the distance and the opening of the joints of the arms.

CONCLUDING THE JI BEN QI GONG

It is important that once you have finished running through the Ji Ben Qi Gong, you close down the energy system correctly and return to a neutral state as shown here.

Bring your feet back to shoulder width and settle your mind. Simply stand and breathe for a while whilst you mentally check your bodily alignments.

After a few breaths turn your hands over towards the sky and begin to inhale. Breathe in as if you are trying to inhale the very essence of the environment. You are now about to run through the 'closing down' exercise which is shown in Figure 4.10.

It is important that the movement of your arms is generated by the opening of the joints of the upper body rather than the biceps as tension here will reduce Qi flow.

Figure 4.10 Closing Down

Bring the arms up high over the head allowing all of the body's joints to open up and 'breathe' with you.

As you reach the peak of your movement, begin to exhale. Bring the arms down in front of your body with the palms facing the floor. Allow your awareness to trace down inside your body as the hands pass you. This will help your consciousness to attach itself to any stagnant energy trapped within your meridian system and lead it down into the ground.

Your hands continue down until they reach your waist. At this point wait and finish your exhalation as your mind traces down through your legs, out the feet and into the floor. This technique is known as Qi Dredging and is a little different from the conventional closing down exercise which Qi Gong practitioners may be used to.

After at least eight repetitions of this exercise you should drop your hands back to your sides.

Let your mind rest within your lower Dan Tien and breathe like this for a few minutes. When you are ready to conclude your training, slowly move your awareness out of your body.

Gently shake out your body and walk briskly for a few minutes. You have now run through the entire sequence of the Ji Ben Qi Gong.

It is suggested that you become very familiar with this exercise set if you wish to begin integrating Nei Gong principles into your regular practice. They are a good set for working through the physical body and then the acquired meridian system. Try practising these exercises for a few weeks until they are remembered within the body's nervous system rather than just your conscious mind. After this begin to refine them by gradually introducing the details outlined in the next chapter where we will look in detail at how to align the various joints of the body and prepare the mind for Nei Gong training.

CHAPTER 5

NEI GONG PREPARATION

Nei Gong is essentially an art form. It is a way of getting in touch with and expressing the nature of our own consciousness. However, before we can reach this level in our training we must first learn the basic rules which underpin our practice. This is the same for any artist; before becoming a great musician you must first learn the various chords and scales relevant to your instrument.

Our physical body is like our workshop. It is here that we work with the various elements of our energy system and eventually our consciousness. If our workshop is a mess then we will produce poor results and so for this reason we must prepare the body for more advanced internal practices.

'Regulate your Qi to soften the body,

Then you may return to the source.'

Our physical body must be in a good state:

- It must be relaxed.

- The joints and bones of the body must be aligned correctly.

- The spaces of our joints must be open and loose.

- The spine must be free and mobile.

- Our health must be of a high standard.

Then we must move on to the nature of our mind and work on this. Our mind must be:

- calm and relaxed

- centred

- focused.

Box 5.1 The Importance of Flexibility

Before practising any form of moving exercise we should warm up the body and stretch; Nei Gong is no exception. Without being loose and flexible in the joints we cannot fully relax the body and Qi flow will be restricted. The importance of stretching is outlined in the *Dao De Jing* and it is an integral element of any internal arts training.

'When we are born we are soft and supple,

When we die we are stiff and hard.

To be soft and flexible is the way of life,

To be rigid and stiff is the way of death.'

The main energy gates of the body (Qi Men) sit within the body's joints. If these areas of the body are tight then Qi, blood and body fluids (Jin Ye) will not be able to flow through and stagnation will occur. Whilst we do not need to be contortionists, we should have a fairly high degree of flexibility which enables us to move comfortably into the various postures of our practices.

Many practitioners of Qi Gong and Taiji shy away from stretching and there is even the opinion that stretching is not required since it is an external method. The fact is that the external cannot be separated from the internal any more than Yin can exist without Yang. If our physical body is not prepared and conditioned correctly then our energy system will suffer. A lack of stretching in Qi Gong and Taiji is a very Western concept. In China it is very rare for any Qi Gong class not to include at least a small amount of preparatory stretching prior to the internal training.

Stretching should be carried out safely and sensibly. If you force your body into extreme positions you will damage yourself. Proceed gently and ensure that you remain in each stretch long enough for your body to fully relax into the posture. Use the Sung breathing method to fully release tension around the joints. Even stretching alone will yield vast improvements to your health, well-being and emotional state. A loose body and happy mindset will provide an excellent foundation for your Nei Gong practice.

An explanation of stretching would take an entire volume in its own right. If you are unsure of how to begin stretching or how to integrate a routine into your daily practice then you might consider going down to your local Yoga class. The various routines and postures you learn here will only serve to benefit your own practice of Nei Gong. I remember being taught very early on in my training that: 'you cannot stretch if you don't relax and you cannot relax if you don't stretch.'

THE INITIAL STAGE OF RELAXING THE BODY

We have already looked at how 'Sung breathing' can be used to release tension from the body whilst in a prone or sitting position. The next stage is learning how to do this whilst moving. The difficulty here is that people have often forgotten how to use their bodies efficiently. Even a simple movement like lifting the arm can generate muscular tension from the abdominal muscles right up to the neck in the majority of people. This is due to the body being out of alignment for one reason or another. Repeated movement with poor postural alignments means that the body has to counter-balance every little movement through contraction of various muscles throughout the body. Our first goal in Nei Gong training must be to retrain our body. We must shed all of the programming which we have gone through over the years and begin to move as we did when we were a child. This reflects the Daoist ideal of 'returning to the source' or 'Ziran'.

The relationship at this stage between relaxing the body through the practice of Sung and learning to correctly align the joints is absolute. You will spend a great deal of time moving between the two processes. They should form an ongoing cycle as shown in Figure 5.1.

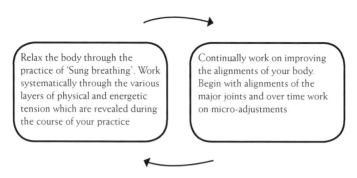

Figure 5.1 The Relaxation/Alignment Cycle

As you relax more into your body, the muscles will ease off and this will allow your bones to shift into a more correct alignment. It is only tension holding you in a bad posture. The difficulty is that when your bones begin to shift, more tension will be created in new muscles as your body begins to work against the change taking place. This means that you have to return to the stage of relaxing and so the cycle repeats itself.

At first this practice will result in large shifts of your physical structure which may result in loud cracking noises. These are nothing to worry about as they will only happen at the early stages in your training. Over time the body's adjustments will become finer and finer until they are almost impossible to feel. It is only as your inner awareness refines that you will become aware of the nature of these micro-adjustments.

Practise these two stages by working through the eight Ji Ben Qi Gong exercises which we covered in Chapter 4. As we have already mentioned, they are based around basic and natural body movements. The various openings and rotations of the joints will enable you to find and release all of the body's major tensions which can be released through your breathing.

Gradually begin to integrate the various alignment principles from this chapter into the eight exercises.

Correct bodily alignments mean that your weight is distributed evenly across the body and bodily fluids can flow unimpeded. The flow of your Qi is also inhibited by incorrect postural alignment as the meridians can become compressed and blocked. It is important to understand that the joints of the body are not designed to support your weight; the skeletal structure is designed to transfer your weight down into the ground so that your joints can function without pressure bearing down on them. If you have incorrect postural habits then your joints will begin to bear too much weight and they will wear out quickly. Many people have joint difficulties when they enter old age and seem to believe this is inevitable. The truth is that our joints are designed to out-live us by a long way and so they should not cause us any problems during the course of our lifetime.

The legs and feet are your body's foundation and so for this reason when training your alignments it is best to start from the floor and work up towards the top of your head.

FEET: THE BODY'S BASE

Your feet are obviously the only parts of your body which are in contact with the floor during the majority of your Nei Gong practice. It is here

that we develop a strong internal connection with the floor. If we are unable to develop this connection then we are reducing the amount of energy which we are able to draw up from the planet and so our internal attainment will be hindered.

Most people carry their body weight in a straight line from their heel up to the top of their head as shown in Figure 5.2.

This in part is due to the manner in which we have evolved. We were originally four-legged animals which evolved to walk upright on two legs. This process of evolution obviously had some major implications for our alignments and body habits, not all of them healthy. One issue is around the line of body weight which drops down from the top of our head into the ground. If we look at an animal's paw, we can see that they do not place the whole of their foot onto the floor and their heel is lifted off the ground. Human legs would be the equivalent of a four-legged animal's rear legs and so Figure 5.3 shows the skeletal structure of a cat's rear legs.

Figure 5.2 Incorrect Line of Body Weight

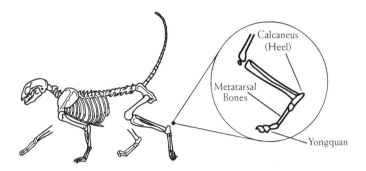

Figure 5.3 Cat's Rear Legs

You can see how the heel is high off the floor and the front part of the foot is in connection with the floor. The animal's body weight is dropped down through the legs into the front part of the foot only. We should emulate this in our Nei Gong practice to a certain degree. Obviously we do not want our heels lifted from the floor as this will uproot us but at the same time we do want the majority of our weight to be held over the front of our feet. Our centre of gravity should move to the spot shown in Figure 5.4.

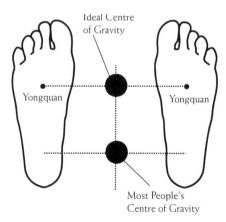

Figure 5.4 The Ideal Position for the Human Centre of Gravity

This may at first seem to contradict the vast majority of teachings in Qi Gong as it may appear that a person must be leaning forward to achieve this. This is in fact not the case and a simple exercise will show you how subtle the movement forward has to be.

Stand in a neutral position with your feet shoulder width apart and facing forwards, as if you were about to practise your Qi Gong exercises. Let your arms hang down by your sides. Carry your body weight over your heels and stand up completely straight.

Now drop your awareness into your lower back and feel what is happening there. You will find that there is a great deal of pressure in the lower spine as it is compacted by the weight of your upper body, tension is stored all around the lower back and midriff.

This is the incorrect position for any form of internal practice. Over time the tension in your lower back will cause your muscles to contract and pull you backwards which leads to the common Qi Gong mistake of leaning backwards.

Now change to the correct position. Shift your body weight forward until you feel the weight begin to move over to the front of your feet. You will notice that it does not take much of a lean forward at all. An onlooker should not be able to see any major change in your posture. If your feet are relaxed enough and you are not wearing tight shoes you will feel that the metatarsal bones will spread apart resulting in your feet feeling slightly wider than before. Your heels should still be touching the floor at this point but there should be very little pressure in them.

If you now move your awareness to your lower back again you will find that the previous pressure there has gone. Your body weight is no longer compressing the spine and so the tension will begin to ease out and the spaces between the vertebrae can begin to open up. You should feel altogether more comfortable in this position.

If you feel that you are leaning too far forwards and that you are unsteady then you have probably gone too far. Spend some time getting used to this position and refining the stance.

So in summary we can see that standing in this manner has brought about two main changes:

- The metatarsal bones of your feet have spread open. On the base of each foot is a very important meridian point known as Yongquan which can be translated as meaning 'Bubbling Spring'. Opening the bones of the front of the foot like this will help to open the Yongquan point. It is the first point on the Kidney meridian and the main point through which we draw the energy of the planet.

- The lower back has freed up and consequently the spine is more relaxed. This helps to open the point known as Mingmen which we will discuss further when we get to the alignment of the spine later in this chapter (see pages 128–133).

Standing in this manner with the weight held in the position shown in Figure 5.4 will gradually help to repair any damage sustained to the lower back over the course of your life as well as increase your vitality as the Kidney meridian is nourished with energy from the planet.

THE LEGS AND PELVIS: THE BODY'S BRIDGE

The legs and pelvis can be compared to a stone bridge. Picture the supporting structure of the stones which hold up a bridge as shown in Figure 5.5.

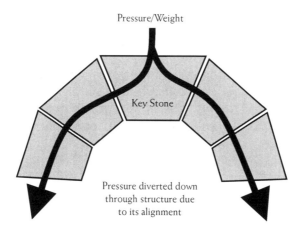

Figure 5.5 The Structure of a Bridge

A bridge built in this way can take huge amounts of downward pressure/weight without collapsing. This is due to the way in which they are aligned with each other as well as the shape of the top stone which is known as the 'key stone'. These stones could even be balanced in place without the need for mortar of any sort and they would still hold.

Figure 5.6 shows how the pelvis is a similar shape to the 'key stone' of a bridge and in the same way it can be used to divert pressure from above down through the legs and into the floor.

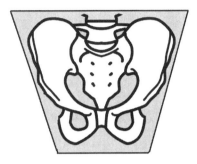

Figure 5.6 The Human Pelvis: Key Stone of the Body

If the lower body is not correctly aligned, you will be able to feel the weight from your upper body in your hips, knees, thighs and calves. The muscles around your hips and legs will have to remain in a state of tension to hold your posture and this will inhibit Qi flow including the Qi which we need to draw from the planet for our practice.

There are two main stances which we use within Nei Gong training. At first they look quite different but in principle they are exactly the same. These two stances are shown in Figure 5.7. You can see that these are the two positions for the lower body which we use within the Ji Ben Qi Gong exercises.

Figure 5.7 Mabu (left) and Wuji (right)

Mabu translates as meaning 'Horse Riding Stance'. It should not only be familiar to those who study Nei Gong but also any Asian martial art. It is the perfect stance for us to practise the alignment of our pelvis and legs so that we emulate the 'arch bridge' structure which will give us so much relaxed stability.

Step out to roughly twice the width of your shoulders as shown in Figure 5.7. Ensure that your feet are facing forwards.

Do not drop too low into this stance. This is a common error which is particularly prevalent in arts like Shaolin and Karate. If your Mabu is any lower than shown in Figure 5.7 you will be out of alignment and so have to rely on muscular tension to hold you in place. If you think back to the structure of the bridge you will see how your weight has to be dropped down through your legs like the curves either side of the 'key stone' which is your pelvis. If the pelvis is dropped too low then your weight will be pressing you down into the space between your legs as shown in Figure 5.8.

Figure 5.8 Incorrect Mabu

At first your Mabu will feel very uncomfortable. The truth is that you are using far too much tension to hold yourself in place. Gradually relax your body using the 'Sung breathing' method. Pay particular attention to the area around your hips and thighs. You should discover that if your body is correctly aligned, the tension will slowly fade away but you should remain in position. With some practice Mabu should begin to feel very relaxed and natural.

It is a common demonstration of stamina and strength in the martial arts to stand in Mabu for a great length of time. Beginners are often amazed by the demonstration but in fact several hours are easy to achieve if you are suitably relaxed and aligned.

Mabu is only really a training exercise within Nei Gong. It is a larger version of the second stance which is known as 'Wuji'. Learning to correct the alignment of the pelvis is easier to do in a larger, more stretched out position. However, it is now time to move on to the smaller stance which is the most common position in Nei Gong.

Bring your feet in to shoulder width apart with your feet facing forwards. Try to repeat the same exercise in this stance. Even though your legs are much closer together, the structural rules of the bridge arch apply here.

You will know when you have managed to attain correct alignment of the pelvis and legs when you experience the following sensations:

- You will suddenly feel very 'buoyant' in your lower body. It is as if your legs have become like water and your body is a bottle floating on this water. If you have ever whiled away some time throwing stones at a bottle floating in a river you will understand the analogy. The bottle (your body) can rock and bounce around in the water but it will always return to floating upright.

- Second you will experience a feeling as if there is a space between the pelvis and the top of your legs. It will seem as if a cushion of air has passed into the space shown in Figure 5.9. Your upper body will feel as if has become completely disconnected from the legs although paradoxically this is actually the start of energetic connection between the upper and lower halves of your body. The area of connection which you are now experiencing is known in Chinese as the 'Kua'.

THE KUA: ENERGETIC CONNECTORS OF THE UPPER AND LOWER
If you can awaken and utilise the Kua correctly you will begin to realise the principle of energetic connection within your training. There is no direct translation of the term 'Kua' into English and so for this reason it has often been left out of teachings that were passed from the East to the West.

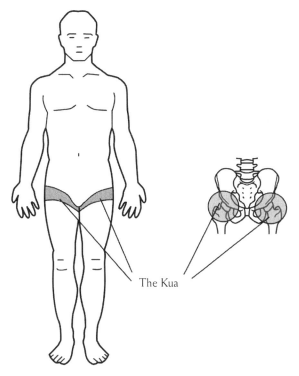

The Kua

Figure 5.9 The Area of the Kua

While the Kua does in part relate to the physical area of your body that exists between your pelvis and the tops of your legs it more accurately refers to the energetic gates which exist in this area. The Qi Men or 'energy gates' are the points in the energy body through which the major flows of Qi pass. They usually exist within the congenital areas of the energy body rather than the acquired although there are some exceptions to this rule.

The Kua are integral to Nei Gong practice as part of their role is to open and close. At first it is hard to distinguish between your physical joints opening and closing and the energy gates opening and closing. In truth, they are both linked and so to a degree opening one will affect the other.

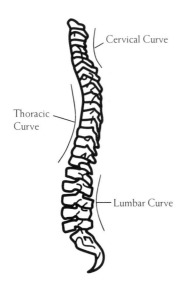

Cervical Curve

Thoracic
Curve

Lumbar Curve

*Figure 5.10 Correct Alignment
of the Human Spine*

THE SPINE: SUPPORTING COLUMN OF THE TORSO

Aligning the spine correctly is of prime importance in your Nei Gong training. It can be particularly difficult due to the fact that there are 25 joints in the length of your back and 24 vertebrae as well as the sacrum. The spine takes a great deal of punishment over the course of a person's life and it is extremely rare to find a person who does not have some sort of vertebral misalignment.

There are numerous theories within the internal arts world as to how the spine should be aligned. These theories range from completely straightening the spine to curling the base of the spine under so that the coccyx points forwards. According to Daoism, alignment of the spine is much simpler. The spine should simply be held in as natural position as possible as shown in Figure 5.10.

The strength and durability of the spine relies on it having the natural curves shown. This position allows the vertebral spaces to be fully opened and the muscles of the back to relax fully. If the spine is straightened or adjusted into an unnatural position it will begin to create tension in the body and unevenly open and close the spaces between the vertebrae. Remember that the idea of Daoism is to adhere to Ziran (a natural state) and this means keeping the snake-like curve of our back.

A common problem with modern people is the misalignment of the pelvis in relationship to the base of the spine. Tension in the lower back causes the muscles to shorten. This pulls the pelvis out of line and tips it into one of two positions. These are shown in Figure 5.11.

The lower back should be relaxed and open with the pelvis 'hanging' from the base of your spine. There is no need to force it backwards or forwards in your training, instead you simply need to relax everything and this will enable the pelvis to hang down into its natural position. The pelvis is shaped like a bowl; if it is aligned correctly it will serve to hold the organs of the lower body. If the lower spine is tense, the tipping of the pelvis will mean that the organs are compressed and held in tension by the muscles of the abdomen. It is quite common for people's digestive disorders to clear up when they are able to sufficiently relax the spine and allow the pelvis to 'hang' down into the correct position.

Figure 5.11 Misalignments of the Pelvis and Lower Back

THE DAOIST SPINAL WAVE

The following exercise will help you to relax your spine and gain full movement across the length of your back. It will ease off the tension in the muscles and begin to bring your spine and pelvis into a healthy alignment.

Stand in a neutral position with your arms hanging loosely by your sides as shown in Figure 5.12.

Next, begin to make circles with your pelvis by dropping a little into your legs, then gently push the pelvis forward and then release it as you rise again so that it returns to a neutral position. What you will end up with is small and gentle circles of the pelvis that will begin to have an effect

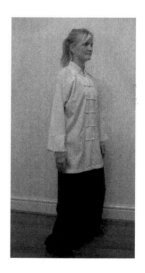

Figure 5.12 Getting Ready to Practise the Daoist Spinal Wave

on the lower part of your lumbar spine. This effect will be a gentle curve appearing at the point in time when the pelvis moves forward. Spend some time making sure that you are comfortable with this stage of practice and that it creates no tension. If it does then shrink the circling of your pelvis until you feel soft again. Figure 5.13 shows the direction of rotation of the pelvis.

Now, let the movement of the lower spine move through your back like a wave until it reaches the base of the skull. It should produce a result similar to the ripple being passed through a whip when it is cracked. Be aware that this exercise should be practised slowly and gently. Any fast movements run the risk of sending a wave up into the neck. This will result in a whiplash injury which can be very painful and detrimental to your practice.

The desired result is a soft 'wave' that moves evenly through the spine and then passes into the neck. At first you will find that your spine only flexes at two or three points. The majority of people will discover that their vertebrae are 'locked' together by the tension in their back. Persevere with this exercise until these 'locked' up vertebrae release and move individually. You are trying to create one smooth movement which is generated by the rotation of the pelvis as shown in Figure 5.14.

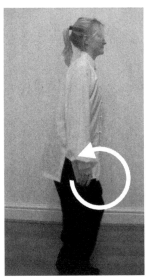
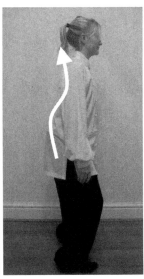

Figure 5.13 Rotating the
Pelvis Forward

Figure 5.14 Spinal Wave

When you are happy that you have achieved an adequate level of spinal flexion then you should continue through the Nei Gong process without focusing on it any more. The spine will be adequately soft and so it will continue to move in this way during your daily training although the movement will now be small enough to be invisible to an observer. Instead you will end up with a body that looks like it is slightly liquefied! You should return to this stage regularly in order to maintain your spinal flexion. I personally spent a long time on this stage when I was learning and now I maintain my spine's health with ten minutes a day when I first get up, prior to meditation. I find that this helps greatly in maintaining my personal health and over the course of a few years your back becomes very strong and flexible.

THE SHU POINTS AND THE MINGMEN AREA

The Bladder meridian runs either side of the spine. It contains several important points known as the Shu points. Shu can be translated as meaning 'to deliver' and so we can see from this that their role is to 'deliver' Qi to various organs of the body. There are Shu points which run to numerous organs and parts of the body. Their location is as shown in Figure 5.15.

The location of the Shu points directly corresponds to the spaces between your vertebrae. If there is tension in the back or the spine is misaligned, the discs which separate the vertebrae become compressed. The vertebrae move together and 'lock' into place which means that the corresponding Shu point is compromised. This restricts the amount of Qi which is led to that particular organ which in turn leads to sickness.

In therapies such as acupuncture and Tui Na it is almost certain that the Shu points will be used in the treatment of most chronic diseases.

Through practice of the Daoist Spinal Wave we will begin to free up the spaces between the vertebrae as described above and so the organs will begin to receive more Qi. From this we can see how working with the spine serves to treat the overall health of the entire body.

The next important part of the energy system which is affected through conditioning the spine is the Mingmen meridian point which is located in the lower back as shown in Figure 5.16.

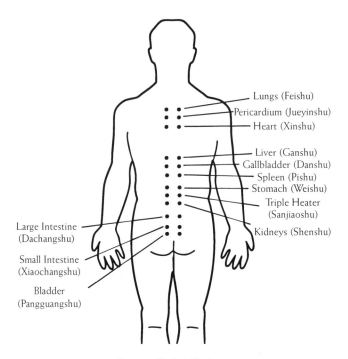

Figure 5.15 The Back Shu Points

Lungs (Feishu)
Pericardium (Jueyinshu)
Heart (Xinshu)

Liver (Ganshu)
Gallbladder (Danshu)
Spleen (Pishu)
Stomach (Weishu)
Triple Heater (Sanjiaoshu)
Kidneys (Shenshu)

Large Intestine (Dachangshu)

Small Intestine (Xiaochangshu)

Bladder (Pangguangshu)

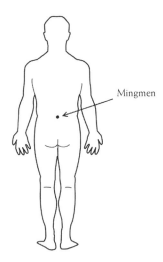

Mingmen

Figure 5.16 Mingmen

Mingmen can be translated as meaning 'The Gateway of your Ming'. This shows us how this particular acupuncture point is directly linked to the state of your Ming which deserves further explanation since it is of prime importance to Daoists. Ming is often translated as meaning your 'destiny or fate'. To me this translation is inadequate due to the connotations we attach to these terms in the West. It is far more accurate to think of your Ming as 'your pre-destined journey from birth to death'.

'Our Ming is to travel from birth to death,

Three in ten follow the natural cause,

Three in ten die of disease or disaster,

Three in ten live well and live long yet they still reach their pre-ordained death.

Why is this?

They aim to extend their time in the transient physical realm.

Only one in ten may achieve the skill of escaping their Ming.'

The inevitably of physical death is a key part of Daoist philosophy. It can be drawn in a chart as shown in Figure 5.17.

Birth ──────────────────────➤ Death

Figure 5.17 The Natural Path of a Person's Ming

Figure 5.17 shows an extremely healthy life whereby a person travelled smoothly into old age, lived a long life and then passed away naturally. In truth it is extremely rare for a human being to achieve this healthy a Ming. The majority of people live unhealthily, experience traumas, grow sick and then deplete their Jing to the point of death early.

According to Chinese medicine the Mingmen meridian point is the source of your Kidney Yin and Yang essence. It is from here that Jing is passed into the lower Dan Tien area and converted into Qi which in turn nourishes the body.

If the Mingmen point is closed up then there will not be such an efficient flow of Jing into the lower Dan Tien area of the body and this will begin to adversely affect your health, immune system and eventually lifespan. Mingmen is also linked to the circulation of Qi in the 'small water wheel' as we will see in Chapter 7.

Freeing up the lower spine and allowing the pelvis to 'hang' into the correct position will assist in the opening of the Mingmen meridian point.

THE SHOULDER BLADES: THE TOP OF OUR ARMS

It is of the utmost importance within Nei Gong training that we connect the whole body together into one unit. This unity of physical structure not only helps to circulate the Qi but on a much simpler level brings about an increase in physical power. If we cannot connect the body together successfully we will never be able to move from our energetic centre which is the key to effective Nei Gong.

In order to understand how to connect the arms in to the body we have to go back to looking at a four-legged animal. Remember that human beings were once roaming the planet on all fours and so some elements of our physical structure still reflect this. Figure 5.18 shows the skeletal structure of a cat.

Scapula (Shoulder Blade)

Figure 5.18 Skeletal Structure of a Cat

Within Daoism it is commonly said that a person should 'move their back as if they were a cat'. This has sometimes been mistranslated as meaning you should keep it arched which only results in tension being created across your upper back and chest. Rather, moving like a cat means that the spine is soft and most importantly you move from the scapula.

The scapula or shoulder blade is the top of our arm. It is much easier to see this on a four-legged animal like the cat shown in Figure 5.18. The scapula is still on top of its body and so when a cat moves, its scapulae rotate and flex to lift and manipulate its front legs. Human beings have now evolved to walk on two legs and consequently our scapulae now rest behind our shoulders. This means that we do not need to use the scapulae to move our arms as we are able to rotate them from the shoulder joint instead. The result is that most people never really use their scapulae and they end up becoming held in place by tension which develops in the muscles and fascia around our back and shoulders. Indeed, when I first ask students who come into my class to move their scapulae around they struggle to move them more than half an inch and this results in a great deal of discomfort after only a few seconds of exercise.

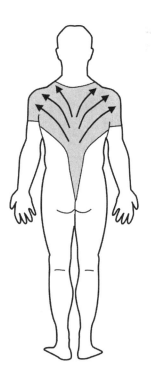

The shoulder blades should be able to move backwards and forwards as well as directly out away from the body. They should still never lift up towards our ears though. The circular movement of the scapulae serves to help open the meridian points around our neck and shoulders as well as to stimulate Qi flow in the two side branches of the thrusting meridian.

Once we are able to move our arms from the scapulae we will have succeeded in connecting the entire body along the line shown in Figure 5.19.

Figure 5.19 The Line of Connection

To free up your scapula, practise the exercise outlined here. It is fairly simple but it is worth practising regularly until you feel that you have full movement in your upper back.

Stand in a neutral position. Lift your arms up in front of you and clasp your hands lightly together as shown in Figure 5.20.

Now slowly draw the scapulae back towards each other as far as they will go, as if you are trying to get them to touch each other in the middle of your upper back.

From here begin to spread the shoulders blades apart as if you are trying to separate the entire body in the direction shown in Figure 5.21. This is very difficult at first but persevere as it will get easier and it is beneficial to your health on numerous levels.

Now bring the scapulae forward as if you are trying to arc your chest as shown in Figure 5.22.

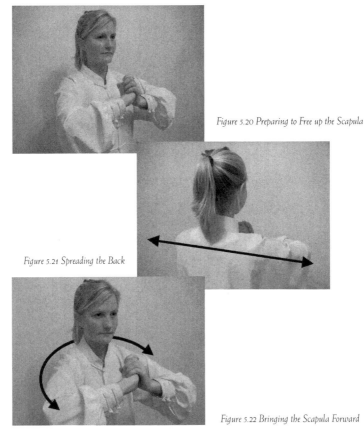

Figure 5.20 Preparing to Free up the Scapula

Figure 5.21 Spreading the Back

Figure 5.22 Bringing the Scapula Forward

From this position relax the scapula back to a neutral position. Then repeat the exercise so that you are circling the scapula. You may well find that this exercise becomes uncomfortable after a short time. After you have finished you may notice a dull ache in the muscles around your back and chest. This is fine, persevere and over a period of time you will notice that the discomfort lessons along with the tension around your scapula.

Obviously when we practise our Nei Gong we should not be moving the scapula to this degree. We are simply exaggerating the movement so that we may free up the muscles. When we carry out movements like those in the Ji Ben Qi Gong the movement of our scapulae should be almost invisible to any onlookers.

Begin moving through the eight exercises outlined in Chapter 4 with your awareness on your arms and scapulae. Try to ensure that you move in the correct manner and see what happens. After some practice you will find that you are able to feel the pull of your muscles and fascia around the area of your lower back; particularly when you lift the arms up to shoulder height. In this way the movement of your arms is starting to open and close the Mingmen area of your spine. If you can achieve this then you are a long way towards connecting the body into a single unit.

THE RELATIONSHIP BETWEEN THE HEAD, THE SPINE AND THE PELVIS

The head, the spine and the pelvis can be thought of as two weights on either end of a chain as shown in Figure 5.23.

Weight A   Weight B

Figure 5.23 Two Weights and a Chain

Weight A can be likened to the skull whilst Weight B is the pelvis. Connecting these two weights is the chain which is your spine.

It is important that when we move up and down in our Nei Gong practice we are always gently teasing open the spaces between the vertebrae so that we are encouraging blood, cerebrospinal fluid and Qi to flow through the length of our spinal column. This serves to nourish the organs, Shu points and brain with vital fluids as well as countless other benefits.

Practise opening the spine by practising the following exercise.

Begin by standing in the neutral position shown in Figure 5.24.

Now begin to squat down from the Kua and hip joints until you are in the position shown in Figure 5.25.

Figure 5.24 Starting to Open the Spine   Figure 5.25 The Squat

Ensure that as you move downwards it is the pelvis that leads you. Remember that the pelvis is like Weight B. It slowly drops straight down and drags the chain which is your spine. The chain then starts to lead the skull downwards.

When you begin to move back upwards you should do the opposite. Your head which is Weight A should lift gently upwards which drags the chain which then leads Weight B up. You should slowly stand back up into the position shown in Figure 5.24.

The important part of this exercise is that the chain must not go slack. If the head leads downwards or the pelvis leads upwards then you will lose the gentle pulling force which is being put onto the spine. Ensure that this exercise is done very gently and slowly so that too much force is not put into the spine. If you are too strong with this practice you may damage your back or neck.

This principle should be integrated into any time you squat or stand in your Nei Gong practice.

OTHER PRINCIPLES OF MOVEMENT

There are numerous other principles of movement and alignment within the internal arts. It would be impossible to list all of them here without the book ending up the size of an encyclopaedia. What I have tried to list here are the principles which I feel are less well understood in the West. For further instruction in the other principles you should head down to your nearest Qi Gong, Taiji or Nei Gong class. The principles are universal across all three of these arts and any good teacher should be able to help you.

It can take a long time to become comfortable with all of the principles outlined in this book. Take your time and gradually layer one principle into your practice at a time. Do not try to practise all of them in one go as you are likely to end up becoming confused; this will lead you nowhere. The trick to any art like this is to progress slowly and steadily.

CONDITIONING THE MIND FOR NEI GONG PRACTICE

The Chinese have a long tradition of linking movements and principles to the characteristics of animals. Their fighting traditions are littered with cranes, tigers and white apes performing all manner of strange techniques.

In the internal arts they talk about two main animals with regards to the human mind. These two animals are the monkey and the horse.

The monkey represents the state of the mind when we begin any meditative or internal practice. Like a monkey, our mind is mischievous and tries to distract us from our practice. It produces hundreds of thoughts continuously and jumps from image to image in an excited fashion. This is the nature of our mind throughout the majority of people's lives until they try to practise something like meditation or Nei Gong. It is only here that we suddenly become aware of the sheer volume of trivial thoughts produced each second by our mind. These thoughts prevent you from ever finding inner stillness.

The horse mind is quiet and steady and an old shire horse. It produces no needless activity. This is the mind we are trying to attain for an art like Nei Gong.

In order to quieten the mind we can use several tricks. These are called 'giving the monkey a banana to appease it'. While the monkey is busy with its banana, it becomes naturally quiet.

The 'banana' we give to our monkey mind can be one of several things depending upon what stage we have reached in our internal development. For example, when practising the initial stages of 'Sung breathing' it is beneficial to follow the movements of our breathing. Whilst this will never entirely quieten the mind, it will slow it enough so that energy from the mind can be redirected into the rest of our body for use within our practice. The process of following the breath is outlined in more detail within Chapter 3.

When you reach the stage of working on alignments you can switch your focus to the various movements and adjustments taking place within your body as you move through the process of change inherent within Nei Gong. Like an interested casual observer you should try to look at what is happening to you as if your body is not really your own. Try to become almost absent minded in your awareness and let your mind trace over your body as you train. If the mind is too strong it will begin to lead Qi to areas of your energy system which can slow your progress at this stage so try to remain casual in your internal observations.

It is fine to use either of these two techniques to calm the mind when practising the Nei Gong exercises outlined within this book. Find which one works best for you. At first this will be nearly impossible as your monkey mind will want to lead your mind away from the practice. Persevere until your mind begins to naturally enter a trance-like state. If you can attain this state of mind whilst still adhering to the principles of Nei Gong then you are progressing well in your practice.

This level of mental conditioning is adequate for this stage in your Nei Gong practice. We will discuss further use of the kind when we begin to get into the more advanced aspects of internal training.

'Acknowledge the Dao and sit in mental quietude,

Cultivate the true consciousness,

This is the way to master the myriad things.'

CHAPTER 6

LOWER DAN TIEN WORK

Progression to working directly with the various elements of the energy body is a stage fraught with false sensations. Although the practices are not actually that difficult, it is important that you are able to discern between a real sign of progression and a physical sensation which has been produced from your imagination. In this chapter we will discuss the early energetic stages of 'converting the Jing to Qi' and 'awakening the energy system'.

Whilst the practices in this section are not as difficult as many teachers would have you believe, they do rely on you having built a strong foundation in the previous stages outlined in this book. If you have not done enough work on conditioning the body and mind then the practices here will yield poor results and your internal development will be seriously hindered. Be honest with yourself and, if unsure, seek the guidance of a qualified instructor who will tell you when it is time to progress.

Working with the physical body can be fairly straightforward. Your body is a tangible entity which can easily be felt during your training. The energy body is obviously a little more difficult to work with, especially for beginners, since it is less tangible than the physical body. The sensations which are signs of progress can be very subtle at first and consequently there is an element of doubt as to what is real and what sensations have been created in your subconscious. This has been a problem since the birth of internal practices and was part of the reason why seeking out a qualified master was an essential part of the training. His or her guidance could save a student a great deal of time which could otherwise be wasted focusing on irrelevances. A second difficulty comes from the fact that most of these teachings were passed down verbally; it is inevitable that some information passed on in this manner will be lost and so over time the available facts became less and less. The few teachings which were put into writing were written in metaphorical language which meant that only the initiated could understand them anyway and so misunderstandings abounded. Some of the major misunderstandings which have now become a major part of contemporary Daoist practices are the sexual practices for which Daoism is well known. The original language of the Daoists was such that it could be taken in numerous ways and one of these ways would be to see the classical texts as referring to the union of a man and woman. Sex may be a natural and healthy part of life but suffice to say that it cannot lead you to enlightenment. The instructions in the classical texts instead referred to Nei Gong practices which helped to prepare the energy body for meditative practices. Indeed sexual practices (but not sex) are seen as a deviant practice within traditional Daoists sects. When we discuss the building up and use of Jing within this chapter we are talking about the base element of creation rather than sexual fluid.

GETTING IN TOUCH WITH YOUR ENERGY BODY

The first challenge to working with your energy body is learning to 'communicate' with it. If you have been practising the exercises and principles within this book for some time already you will probably have had some experiences of the energy body. There may have been subtle sensations of heat, pressure or vibration within your body as you ran through the Ji Ben Qi Gong exercises or in particular the 'Sung breathing' exercises. If you have already managed to tune in to the movements of the energetic field during your breathing practice and released tensions from the energy body then you are already able to tune in to the energy body to some degree. If you can't by this time then do not worry, we will look now in detail at the nature of the lower Dan Tien which is the easiest way to begin feeling your energetic body.

'This is the way of the sage:

He empties his Heart-Mind,

Gazes into his belly and rids himself of desires.'

The lower Dan Tien is situated roughly three inches below the navel within the core of your lower abdomen as shown in Figure 6.1.

The lower Dan Tien is the driving force of change and movement within the energy body; some sects of Daoism even consider it to be the only Dan Tien. They completely ignore the existence of the middle and upper Dan Tien.

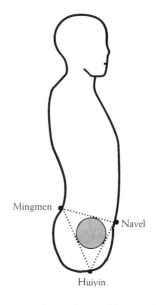

Figure 6.1 Location of the Lower Dan Tien

The lower Dan Tien carries out several important functions including the conversion of Jing to Qi as well as the circulation of Qi throughout the meridian system but for now we only need concentrate on its third function: that of 'tuning' the mind into the frequency of the energy body.

Within Daoist alchemical texts there are a great many references to the Kan and Li trigrams which are shown in Figure 6.2.

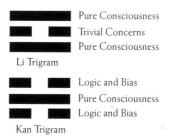

Pure Consciousness
Trivial Concerns
Pure Consciousness
Li Trigram

Logic and Bias
Pure Consciousness
Logic and Bias
Kan Trigram

Figure 6.2 Kan and Li

With regard to this stage in the Nei Gong process Kan and Li represent the state of our mind when we are in unenlightened state. It has long been said within Chinese thought that there are three locations within the body where thoughts can be processed. These are as follows:

• The mind, which resides within the brain. Western science would agree that this is the location for human thought.

- The heart or location of the middle Dan Tien is said to be the location where emotional information and thoughts are processed.

- The guts or area of the lower Dan Tien. According to Eastern thought this is the area of the body from which a great deal of our intuitive information is processed into thought. We have also known this in the West for a long time; we have all heard people talk about 'gut feelings' after all.

The Li trigram shown in Figure 6.2 represents the state of the consciousness which sits within our mind. This is the house of the upper Dan Tien. This part of our consciousness deals with our day-to-day thought processes which enable us to function on a daily basis. We can see that it is the trigram of 'Fire'. It is represented by two unbroken 'Yang' lines which are surrounding a broken 'Yin' line. The two Yang lines are the energy of pure consciousness, the enlightened thought which is nourished by the energy of Heaven in Daoist cosmology.

Human beings would be able to communicate with the very energy of Heaven if not for one problem, the infiltration of trivial concerns. If we were able to shed the mundane thoughts and concerns from our mind we would attain a sudden state of pure Yang consciousness which would reunite the mind with Heaven. This can be likened to the two states of the monkey mind and the horse mind which we discussed in Chapter 5.

It is the trivial thoughts which prevent us from feeling and understanding the nature of our energetic body and then ultimately our innate wisdom.

The Kan trigram has two broken 'Yin' lines which surround a solid 'Yang' line. The Yang energy of pure consciousness is representative of our 'gut feelings': the sixth sense which provides us with the knowledge that something is amiss deep within our lower abdomen. Unfortunately this intuitive wisdom is buried between two Yin lines of logic and bias.

Logic and bias are obviously useful to us on a daily basis. Logic and bias inform our decision making and how we function in life. Without logic people would behave like newborn children for their entire lives. The problem with logic and bias is that they have been taught to us by others. Our parents and peers slowly taught us how to think and what was right and wrong; we have been through the education system and then of course added our own learning from the experiences we have had. All of this acquired knowledge over-writes our 'gut feelings' and so we start to lose the ability to 'know things' intuitively at a young age.

'It is difficult to master yourself with learnt knowledge,

Gained knowledge will bring ruin,

Intuitive wisdom is the way to good fortune.'

This state of mental being is what prevents us from feeling our inner self. We are limited to the physical realm with the exception of our emotions which we will look at in further detail when we cover advanced practices in Chapter 8 (page 191).

The Daoists developed a very simple method of undoing these issues temporarily so that we may 'tune' into the energy body during our practice. Although the theory may be complex, the practice is actually very straightforward. This method was known as 'inverting Kan and Li'. This term appears in many classical texts. It should not be confused with terms such as 'reversing Fire and Water' or 'merging Kan and Li' though, as these refer to different stages in Daoist internal alchemy.

Inverting Kan and Li means to drop our mental awareness down into the region of the lower Dan Tien. The mental awareness of our mind is directly linked to our sense faculties and so we can use these to connect to the energy contained within our lower abdomen. This results in the following process taking place.

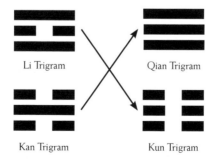

Li Trigram   Qian Trigram

Kan Trigram   Kun Trigram

Figure 6.3 Inverting Kan and Li

In the diagrammatical representation of the shift in consciousness, the central lines of the Kan and Li trigrams have become reversed. This results in the creation of the Qian (Heaven) and Kun (Earth) trigrams.

The Qian trigram over the Kun trigram is the representation of a congenital state of consciousness: one who has managed to still the mind and shed all of the mundane thoughts and conditioned thinking which kept him from realising the universal truth. This does not mean that you have attained enlightenment though! It is a little more involved than simply putting your mind on to the lower Dan Tien. Placing your awareness successfully onto the area of the lower Dan Tien does, however, enable you to still your mind to such a state that it begins to tune in to the frequency of the energy body. This can take some time so please be patient and take some time working on the following methods; experiment and then select the one which you feel works best for you.

- Try to feel the location of the lower Dan Tien. Let your awareness hover over the area of the lower abdomen and search for the field of energy that sits there. This is the method which is traditionally used within Daoist schools but in all honesty I believe it only works for a very small percentage of people.

- Use your hearing. Listen for the sound of the lower Dan Tien. This might sound a little odd but if you are patient enough you will begin to hear an audible noise emanating from within the lower abdomen. Once you have picked up the sound of the lower Dan Tien you can 'follow' it with your hearing in the same way that you might focus on a distant sound to discover which direction it is coming from. Obviously this relies on practising your Nei Gong in a quiet room as any outside noise can trick you into thinking you have located the lower Dan Tien. The sound of the lower Dan Tien can vary from person to person but it is usually described as being like waves crashing on the ocean although in my own experience it sounds more like a low humming piece of machinery.

- Use physical landmarks to locate the lower Dan Tien. The lower Dan Tien exists directly above the Huiyin meridian point and the perineum. We can use this to help us in our practice. Drop your awareness down into your perineum. Gradually begin to lift the perineum on each inhalation; this should give you a distinct location for your mind to attach to. Many people are surprised at just how far from this location they were focusing. It is a common error for students to focus on their belly or in front of their lower abdomen outside their belly without realising. Once you have found this location you may stop lifting the perineum and rest your mind an inch or so above this point until the lower Dan Tien is discovered.

- The last method involves using a visualisation. This is recommended only for those whose minds are very 'image based'. Personally this is the only method I have had no luck with but several of my students have stated that this method works very well for them. Picture a Taiji symbol (Figure 6.4) in the lower abdomen three inches below the navel. Spend some time creating the image and try to focus on every detail. This should help still the mind as it has something creative to focus upon. Over time your mind should naturally begin to attach itself to the actual location of the lower Dan Tien and then the image will no longer be required. This is another common method within Daoism but I should point out that I think it is flawed since I feel that it runs the risk of engaging the practitioner's imagination which is detrimental to your practice. Try it though if you think that it might work for you.

Figure 6.4 Taiji Symbol

Regular practice will soon bring results at this stage in your Nei Gong training. You will know when you have managed to locate the lower Dan Tien when you begin to feel the conversion of the Jing to Qi taking place within your lower abdomen.

THE CONVERSION OF JING TO QI

We already looked briefly at the nature of Jing and its relationship to Qi and Shen within Chapter 2 when we discussed energetic anatomy. It is important to keep in mind that the three substances are really just three different vibrational frequencies that can be changed easily into each other if the frequency is changed. The vibrations are each capable of carrying information and so the mind will translate this information into various different sensations and experiences. Jing quite clearly produces the sensation of heat within the body. This is different from the heat which is produced from regular Qi Gong training which is caused by an increase in blood flow across the body.

The heat of Jing is a very intense heat that feels much like you have a fresh hot water bottle pressed against your body. A few minutes of intense Jing movement will result in your body being drenched in sweat. Students who have been to this stage in my classes have been shocked at how wet they find their clothes have become after only a short time moving their Jing through internal practices. I am happy to say that this experience only lasts for a short time. As is the case with all sensations within Nei Gong, the body soon becomes used to it and so it becomes normal. This means that the sensation dies down in intensity and becomes far more subtle.

'Within the darkness of Dao lay hidden the original Jing.

When cultivated, the Jing contains the potential for existence.'

The Jing will move from the Mingmen area of your back through to the lower Dan Tien and genital region of your body. It is here that it begins to transform into Qi. For a period of time you will not be aware of this conversion process though as your mind will still be adjusting to the movement of the Jing. It is also unlikely at this early stage that you will be able to feel the path of the Jing as it runs from the small of your back to the lower abdomen. Instead you will feel the heat as it develops within the lower Dan Tien and then gradually spreads around the genitals, hips and belly.

NOTES ON WORKING WITH THE JING

It is suggested within numerous classical texts including the Suwen (theoretical questions on the nature of organic life), which is part of the oldest book on Chinese medicine, that Jing conservation is of utmost importance for long life and good health. Daoist schools of thought recommend various practices which aid in the conservation of Jing.

Box 6.1 Yang Shen Fa

Yang Shen Fa is the study of healthy living. This should be an important concern for those who study the internal arts. The most important aspect of Yang Shen Fa is a study of your diet. Your body requires a healthy supply of nutrients in order to create the Qi which nourishes your organs. Without this you will be limited in your practice and even the simplest internal exercises will leave you feeling tired.

The study of nutrition is a long and complex subject. There are countless books available on healthy eating and you should look into the guidance they give. An excellent author is Daniel Reid. His books can easily be bought from the internet and many bookstores. They contain a wealth of information on healthy eating as well as numerous other aspects of Yang Shen Fa among other subjects.

It is important to understand that practising Nei Gong will greatly increase your body's sensitivity to outside factors including the quality of your food. This means that unhealthy food such as processed or convenience food will have a far greater effect on you than it did before you started to study Nei Gong. Whereas you might not have noticed the effects of a pizza before, you will now find that you become sick, tired and often have loose bowels shortly afterwards. The body will seek to eject the toxic food from your system. Your body will also dislike extremely cold food such as ice cream which should be completely cut out of your diet. My students also find that they become intoxicated on even a very small amount of alcohol and their hangovers last for several days. Most of them quickly quit drinking.

None of these affect you because of the Nei Gong, rather they always affected you this way but you were unaware. Practising Nei Gong gives you a greater connection to what is happening within your body and brings to the surface what previously went unnoticed.

Smoking should also be cut out as soon as possible. This has hugely detrimental effects on your health as well as your Nei Gong training. If you are not used to China it is quite horrifying to see just how many of their Qi Gong and Taiji teachers puff away on cigarette after cigarette whilst teaching in the parks!

For now it is enough to be familiar with a few key guidelines which are best to keep in mind when reaching this stage in your Nei Gong training:

- First, you need to look closely at the food you eat. Your body needs to be strong and healthy for this kind of internal work and so for this reason you should eat a healthy diet. Limit the amount of sugar you eat, cut out as much spicy food as you can and definitely stay away from processed foods like fast food and takeaways. Your diet should be balanced and nutritious; it is not a rule that you need to be vegetarian but you should restrict your meat consumption to maybe one meal every week at the most.

- Sexual intercourse drains the Jing more than anything else, particularly in men. When you are beginning the conversion of Jing to Qi you need to limit your sexual activity as this will seriously hinder your progress. It often states within alchemical texts that a person should abstain from sex for a hundred days prior to practising these methods; this guideline is okay but there are other dangers inherent here such as disharmony within the household! Just be sensible but if you need a guideline look for any discomfort or tightening in the lower back or knees after sex. If you have either of these symptoms then you are over-straining the kidneys through Jing depletion and this can be damaging to your health. The amount of sexual activity that you can safely engage in varies according to age. Usually it is said that a person in their teens may have sex once a day, in your twenties once every three days, in your thirties once a week and in your forties once a fortnight and so on. These guidelines are healthy if you are practising Nei Gong.

- Jing is linked to your immune system so do not practise this technique when you are feeling unwell as this will damage your health.

- Do not practise if you are over-tired as this will speed up Jing depletion.

- Cut out all alcohol when working on this stage in your practice and never combine Nei Gong with drugs of any sort, especially hallucinogens.

- This is a guideline which I am adding since it would not have been relevant until recently. Limit or cut out completely the television, internet and mobile phones when you begin this stage in your practice. You are trying to get in touch with a refined vibrational frequency which is your energy body. Unfortunately the three aforementioned items give off their own frequencies which affect the energy system and mind. They will interfere with your practice and dull your awareness. I personally cannot practise meditation in the vicinity of a television, computer or mobile phone since the vibrations send an uncomfortable feeling of pressure into my body.

- Do not practise this method if you are pregnant as it may be damaging to your unborn child. There is even the risk that it may abort your pregnancy. If you are keen on practising Nei Gong and you are pregnant, take the opportunity to work on your alignments for a solid nine months.

- The heart is particularly sensitive to internal heat. If you have any sort of heart problems or high blood pressure then please proceed carefully. You should not allow the heat to build up to any more than a gentle warmth. If you start to sweat profusely as described above then stop your practice and wait until the heat resides. You are going to have to progress much more slowly than those with a healthy heart. I highly recommend that you find a qualified teacher who can guide you safely through this part of the process.

It is a common concern that this practice in itself drains vital Jing which reduces your health and lifespan. This is not true as long as you practise sensibly. Your awareness must be gentle just as it has been in all of the other practices which we have covered up until now. Remember to treat the whole of Nei Gong as though your mind were a casual observer. If you keep this level of focus you will simply tune into a process which is naturally taking place all of the time. Your awareness will not affect it in any way other than to refine the process and make it more efficient which is the key. At this stage we are simply looking for a way to feel and understand the workings of the energy body.

If your focus is too strong you will find that the practice leaves you tired and you will suffer stiffness and bruising in the lower back around the kidneys. In this case you should soften your focus in your next practice session. A few times with this error will do you no major harm but several years in this manner will indeed start to drain the Jing faster than is healthy.

You may practise connecting to the lower Dan Tien and becoming aware of the conversion of Jing to Qi in any one of the eight Ji Ben Qi Gong but to be honest it is easier to do so whilst sitting down or lying on your back. There is enough to focus on for the time being without trying to perform external movements as well. Only when you have a strong feel for the heat at this stage should you begin to integrate the practice into moving exercises.

HOW LONG TO CONTINUE WITH THIS PRACTICE

At first you are only able to feel physical sensation; after practising this method for some time you are able to tune into the vibration frequency of your Jing as we have described above. You should continue with this stage until you are able to start feeling the existence of Qi in the lower belly. This is a sign that the awareness of your mind has refined further and is now able to tune into the frequency of Qi.

Like Jing, Qi is also a vibration wave that carries information. Your mind translates this information into the sensation of internal movement when it is within the body. When your mind is becoming aware of Qi in this area you will feel a subtle movement within the lower Dan Tien which feels much like water bubbling. This bubbling will be subtle at first but then gradually increase until it is a steady vibration which feels much like a car engine ticking over. It even increases to the point whereby your lower abdomen quivers and even shakes quite sharply. These shakes are often visible to an onlooker. At first they come in short bursts but after a while they settle down into a smooth and steady 'buzz' which shrinks down until you can feel it only in the lower Dan Tien itself.

To start the movement of Qi within the lower abdomen you need to have built a very strong foundation in the previous stages outlined in earlier chapters. Your alignments need to be very exact and your body must be soft and open. You also need to have developed a strong awareness of your Jing and felt a great deal of heat in the lower abdomen. It is safe to say that the majority of Qi Gong practitioners never reach this stage as they do not spend enough time practising; Nei Gong is a life study and the amount of commitment required is too much for most people. Those seeking only health benefits and a little relaxation have no need to aim for this stage in their practice; the stages outlined up to this point will adequately meet these needs and require considerably less practice time.

It is at this time that you can begin to end your practice and move on to the next stage in your training which is the 'awakening of the energy system'. Before we move on to look at this area of Nei Gong it is wise to look at various mistakes that can arise within your practice and the associated risks. Please note that these risks are extremely small and problems arising at this level in the training are very rare. However, I feel it is important to look briefly at these risks since very little is currently written on them in the West.

QI STAGNATION

Qi stagnation in the lower abdomen can be caused by an excessively strong focus over a long period of time. Qi will begin to stay within the lower Dan Tien and the result is that your lower abdomen will begin to bloat. You will gradually gain weight until you have a pronounced 'pot belly'. This can also be caused by focusing your awareness on the lower Dan Tien long after it is needed. If you are not aware of the process of tuning the mind into the movement of the Jing and instead simply keep your mind on the lower Dan Tien you will prevent the Qi from moving into the rest of the meridian system. At first the problem is no worse than a little bloating but after several years it can stiffen the entire body and then lead to digestive disorders and sexual dysfunction. The danger is that some schools teach that the bloating of the belly is a good sign since it indicates a strong amount of Qi in the lower Dan Tien; this is simply not true.

A slight 'pot belly' can be caused by deep abdominal breathing, especially if you had previously built up strong abdominal muscles through a practice such as external martial arts but this should cause a much smaller degree of bloating than Qi stagnation.

DRAGON SICKNESS

Dragon sickness is a rather scary name for a rather serious condition which can be caused by incorrect Qi Gong practice. It can occur at any stage in the practice. Dragon sickness develops when the mind develops too much of an attachment to the movements of the energy body and in particular its external manifestations which are the emotions.

Dragon sickness shares a lot of similarities with mental illnesses such as psychoses and schizophrenia. Sufferers may experience dramatic changes in mood over a short period of time that range from deep suicidal depression through to intense rage. Hallucinations may also start to develop and sufferers may hear voices in their head.

There are some groups that actually aim to develop these symptoms as they believe that the symptoms are the signs of immortals speaking to them from the enlightened realm. I encountered one such group of Taiwanese practitioners who were incredibly sick and totally oblivious to what was happening; they had a very dominant teacher who was revered as a god by his students. Luckily these groups do not seem to exist in the West as far as I am aware.

It is highly unlikely that you will manifest dragon sickness if you adhere to the principles of safe practice and watch out for the following signs that something is wrong with your practice. If you find that you are starting to experience heightened states of mania, depression or anger then immediately stop your practice. It is common to experience these states to a small degree later in your practice as the emotions move into balance but the emotional shifts linked to incorrect practice are far more intense and totally out of your control. If you get to the stage of having hallucinations or intense headaches that feel like a white-hot burning deep in the brain then you should end all internal training. In both cases seek out a highly experienced practitioner who can help you; under no circumstances start your practice again until you have had treatment.

I should also add that dragon sickness is more likely to appear in a practitioner who has a tendency towards some sort of mental illness already. If you suffer from any mental illnesses you should ensure that you let your teacher know and consider seeking treatment before engaging in any internal practices. Nei Gong should never be used instead of conventional therapies.

AWAKENING THE ENERGY BODY

It is at this point in the training that we have gone beyond the realms of what is possible through standard Qi Gong training alone. The techniques from here may be considered advanced internal practices although in the grand scheme of Nei Gong they are still only building the foundation for the higher practices.

Every person's energy system is functioning throughout their entire life. If this energy system were to suddenly stop working they would quite simply die; what does differ is how efficiently it runs. The level of efficiency depends on several things including how tense your physical body is, how blocked the various pathways of the meridian system are, how balanced your emotional state is and to what degree the physical and energetic bodies are integrated. There are of course countless other factors determining how efficiently your energy body is running but for the purposes of Nei Gong we only really need concern ourselves with the above list.

When awakening the energy system we need to ask ourselves the following questions:

- Is my physical body relaxed? Have I opened up my joints and softened my body through 'Sung breathing'? If the answer is no then you need to return to the earlier practices before attempting to awaken the energy system.

- Are my energetic pathways blocked? If your energetic pathways are fairly opened up then you should have a high degree of health and mobility in your body. If not then spend more time working on exercises like the Ji Ben Qi Gong until you reach this state. Practices like Taiji or meditation can also be of great help here. As any practitioner of Chinese medicine will tell you, it is almost impossible to completely open up the entire meridian system and free it of every blockage; we are just trying to get as close as we can to this point. Use your common sense and seek the advice of an experienced teacher if you feel unsure.

- Are my emotions fairly well balanced? Only enlightened beings are completely harmonious in their emotional state but there are degrees as to how much you swing between your moods and feelings. If you tend to suffer from strong

> feelings of depression, rage, mania, etc. then you need further
> self-development work before you move on to awakening the
> energy system. A calm and clear mind is needed.

Integration of the physical and energetic bodies will begin to take
place as we awaken the energy system. We will discuss this part of the
process in further detail in this chapter.

Awakening the energy system means stimulating Qi movement
through the various pathways of the meridian system. Qi, of course,
already travels through these pathways but through our practices we
are aiming to increase the efficiency of this process. In order to help us
understand how this happens we should look at the nature of what a
meridian is in further detail.

Human beings are vibrating entities. If we ceased to vibrate we
would cease to exist; movement is the key to life. We vibrate on various
levels right from the matter which makes up our tissue, through to
our cells, molecules and eventually the energy which we the Chinese
simply called Qi. These small 'particles' of Qi vibrate in a completely
random manner. At their innermost level human beings are complete
chaos. These 'particles' of Qi bounce and clash into each other with
seemingly no rhyme or reason.

Within all of this chaos exist several lines of Qi which do not join
in the chaos which surrounds them. Instead they vibrate in a general
direction as shown in Figure 6.5.

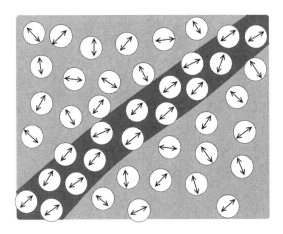

Figure 6.5 The Behaviour of Qi

If you look at Figure 6.5 you can see how the various particles of what we simply call Qi vibrate backwards and forwards in all directions around their own small area. Down the middle of the diagram is a line of Qi which all vibrate in the same direction; this line is marked out with the darker grey colour behind them. This line of vibration which is all moving in the same direction is what we know as a meridian. This is of course only a diagrammatical representation; in actuality a meridian has far more than just two particles of Qi across its width.

If we think back to the nature of what Qi is, we have talked about it being a wave of vibrating energy which can carry information which is stored in a similar way to binary code. Refer back to Chapters 1 and 2 for more details on this (see pages 30–31 and 69). This wave of information is passed along the line of vibrating Qi which is moving in the same direction and this is what the ancient Daoists called 'Qi flow along a meridian'.

How are these meridians formed? They are constructed from the power of consciousness. In the process of creation the energetic realm is created from the realm of consciousness which was also known as the realm of Heaven. We mentioned this in Chapter 1 when we stated that:

The Realm of Consciousness

Gives birth to

The Energetic Realm

Which gives birth to

The Physical Realm

It is this very nature of the meridians that enables us to work with them through Nei Gong practice. Our consciousness can, with time, begin to affect the movement of Qi along the meridians if we are able to combine it with our breath and send a new directional force along the line of the existing energetic pathway. A blockage within the meridian is just the opposite from what we want; a piece of negative information generated by an accident or illness; this disrupts the normal direction of the vibration along the meridian and so some of the particles of Qi begin to vibrate in a chaotic manner like the Qi which surrounds the meridian. Information that passes along this line is now disrupted and so 'Qi flow is disrupted'. A therapy such as acupuncture seeks to access these pathways of information and repair the direction of vibration. A skilled acupuncturist will use his or her needle to access the meridian and then use mental intent or Yi to access the meridian and begin to redirect the vibrating Qi so that the patient begins to get well. This can also be accomplished by skilled massage therapists if they are able to use their intention to a high level.

So awakening the energy system means to increase the efficiency of the meridians through affecting the alignment of the vibrating Qi. If we are able to affect more of the Qi which surrounds the meridian and get it to move in the same direction then we are able to pass more information effectively along this pathway and so the flow of Qi is strengthened. It is important that we use a gentle intent to pass along this line though; if we use too strong a focus then we will disrupt the vibrating Qi and send it vibrating chaotically. In this way the excessively strong intention has created more blockages. It is for this reason that we do not try to access each meridian directly with our mind. Instead we use the lower Dan Tien as a driving force.

Those who are interested in exploring this concept further should investigate systems of meditation under the guidance of a qualified teacher. This is because there are two skills gained from meditation known as 'outer' and 'inner' vision. The names may vary slightly from system to system but the effect is the same. Outer vision allows your consciousness to leave your body and travel to any location on the planet during your meditation; this skill is also known as astral projection. Unfortunately I have, to this date, never shown any aptitude for this skill which is a real shame since it sounds like a marvellous thing to experience. I have had, however, good results with regards to inner vision. This is the ability to send your gaze into your own physical or energy body and zoom in to any degree you wish. In the past, ancient Daoists were able to examine the world using this skill and knew about bacteria, cells and molecules long before the invention of the microscope. When you manage to look directly at your own meridian system you will see the truth in the description above. The various particles of Qi shine with a bright light and bounce around chaotically. From slightly further out the meridians look like a network of white threads amongst the rest of your energy body which I can only conclude is due to the passing of mental information, in the form of Shen, along their length.

THE DRIVING FORCE OF THE LOWER DAN TIEN

Qi naturally travels through our meridians throughout the course of our daily lives. We do not have to use mental intention to decide the direction of Qi; instead it takes place on a purely automatic and subconscious level. This is due to two factors: our breathing and our lower Dan Tien. We have already seen how our breathing affects the internal pressure in the abdominal cavity. For more information on this please refer to Chapter 3 when we looked at 'Sung Breathing' (pages 77–78). The pressure change in the abdominal cavity serves to stimulate the field of pure energetic information we call the lower Dan Tien. The Dan Tien is then gently kept rotating; it completes a single rotation in 24 hours. The direction of its rotation is dictated by the girdling meridian which dips slightly on the front of your body (see Chapter 2, page 60). The rotation of the lower Dan Tien serves as the catalyst for the movement of Qi through the meridians which is driven smoothly around your energy body. This process is summarised in Figure 6.6.

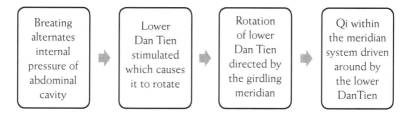

Figure 6.6 Process of Qi Circulation

The Daoists called the various circulations of Qi within the body the 'small water wheels of Qi'. The Dan Tien is the water wheel itself which runs the system of Qi circulation. For our Nei Gong practice we now need to work with the efficiency of the lower Dan Tien and manually take control of its rotation for a short period of time. Once we have improved its effectiveness we will return the control of the lower Dan Tien to our subconscious where it will continue to run under the control of our breathing.

The Taiji symbol which we have already mentioned several times in this book is familiar to most people. What is not so well known is that there are several different versions of the Taiji symbol and that they all have different meanings. Within the macrocosm of the universe these symbols are representative of the different stages of movement and creation manifested by the force of Taiji. Within the microcosm of our body there are various degrees of Dan Tien rotation. Three of the most important Taiji symbols are shown in Figure 6.7.

A   B   C

Figure 6.7 Taiji Symbols

Symbol A shows a steady rotation of the lower Dan Tien which takes place over a 24-hour period. This is the natural state of the lower Dan Tien which takes place in an average healthy person. It is due to this steady rotation that Qi circulation is stronger within different meridians at different times of the day. This is more relevant to Chinese medicine than Nei Gong and so you should refer to any good acupuncture text book for more details on this.

Symbol B shows a slightly stronger rotation which is a little faster. This symbol is prevalent within many Daoist monasteries within China and is representative of the Nei Gong practices which once took place there. Unfortunately the persecution of the internal arts which took place during the Cultural Revolution all but ended these practices. This symbol is the state of rotation which we are aiming for in the lower Dan Tien now.

Symbol C shows a very advanced practitioner's lower Dan Tien. It shows the Dan Tien rotating smoothly into the emptiness of Wuji which sits at the centre of the circle. This is the state of 'no regulation' whereby the Nei Gong process happens automatically. There is no longer a need to do any internal work other than to sit by and watch the internal transformation taking place. This symbol is also very common within the Daoist monasteries of China and Daoist classical texts.

You should already have managed to locate the lower Dan Tien and should be able to feel the low vibration which is taking place within its centre. If you have not reached this stage in your development then you will find this next exercise almost impossible. Return to the previous exercises as you have not yet built a strong enough foundation.

ROTATING THE LOWER DAN TIEN

Place your mind within the centre of your lower Dan Tien and let it settle there for some time.

Now begin to turn the Dan Tien forward using your mind as shown in Figure 6.8.

This is the most natural direction of rotation for the Dan Tien as it drives the Qi up the governing meridian and down the conception meridian. This is the main small water wheel of Qi which serves to regulate Qi flow within the rest of your energy body.

At first it will be very difficult to turn the Dan Tien with your mind and you may be tempted to give up. Just stick with it and over time you will find that you are able to turn it forward in a smooth rotation. Turn it slowly and steadily; co-ordinate the rotation with your breathing so that one turn of the Dan Tien is timed with one cycle of breathing in and out.

Starting to try and move the lower Dan Tien is like trying to gain control of a new limb. If you suddenly woke up this morning to discover that you had grown a third arm it would probably just hang lifelessly at your side. Your mind and nervous system would not yet know how to link to the new arm and so it would take a long time before you had full control over its movement. The lower Dan Tien is the same. It will take some time before your consciousness knows how to move it in the direction you want.

When the lower Dan Tien begins to turn it will feel a little strange. It has been likened by several of my students to a fish turning over in their stomach. To be honest I am a little perplexed as to how they know what this feels like but I can understand what they mean. It is not altogether a pleasant feeling at first but your body soon gets used to it and then the feeling becomes much more subtle. There are a few

Figure 6.8 Rotating the
Lower Dan Tien

side effects to the initial rotation of the lower Dan Tien which are nothing to worry about. They are a temporary part of the process of awakening the energy system and should not last long. These are as follows:

- As the lower Dan Tien sits within the lower abdomen, it has direct effects on the lower digestive system. Many people have a great deal of stagnant fluids and toxins sitting within their digestive system, of which they are unaware. This is caused by a combination of acid-forming foods and negative emotions. When the lower Dan Tien starts to turn it can cause a short period of nausea and even vomiting as these toxins are removed from the body. This should not last more than a few days at the most.

- The human colon is inevitably full of no end of waste matter which is left over from our increasingly unhealthy diet in modern times. This waste matter slowly builds up until it creates no end of physical problems for us in later life. Fasting has long been an important part of many spiritual traditions including Daoism where it is known as 'Bigu'. When the lower Dan Tien begins to turn it often flushes some of this material out of the colon through a burst of diarrhoea which can last for up to a week. Having completed periods of fasting and colonic cleansing myself I can reliably report that the matter which comes out of your body when the lower Dan Tien begins to rotate is the same as the matter which comes out of you during a colonic cleanse.

- If women practise the rotation of the lower Dan Tien during their menstrual cycle it can cause a slightly increased flow of menstruation due to the increase in blood and energy flow. If this happens, women should stop the practice and wait until they have finished their cycle.

Please do not worry if any of the above side effects take place. They are a completely natural part of the Nei Gong process and should only last for a short period of time. If they last any longer, go and see a practitioner of Traditional Chinese Medicine; rotation of the lower Dan Tien may well have brought to the surface an imbalance which was previously unknown to you.

Spend some time working only on this direction of rotation. I suggest that you spend a portion of time on this direction every day for a few months at the minimum until you are satisfied that you have attained a smooth and healthy forward rotation. Ensure that you only work with the lower Dan Tien in this way. The middle and upper Dan Tien affect your brain waves and emotions. Conscious rotation of these energy centres is not advised; I myself experimented with this and did not have a particularly pleasant time.

INDUCED QI FLOW AND SPONTANEOUS ENERGETIC MOVEMENT

When we rotate the lower Dan Tien it drives information throughout the body which begins to adjust the direction of vibration along the meridians. This increases the efficiency by which they transfer Qi through the body. This is known as an 'induced Qi flow'. This has several effects as the energy body and physical body begin to co-ordinate with each other. The nervous system is affected for a short period of time and we often get a natural phenomenon known as 'spontaneous energetic movement'. This is where the practitioner's body begins to move in strange and uncontrollable ways which can be very amusing both to experience and to watch.

'Who can sit in quietude and allow the waters to clear?

Clearing the waters leads to a new and spontaneous movement.'

Spontaneous energetic movement is a controversial subject within the internal arts world which is often shrouded in mystery and misinformation. There are also sinister aspects to it whereby an unscrupulous teacher will tell his students that it is the power of god working through his students. Inevitably a great deal of money changes hands and the teacher enjoys his position of power over the group. It is important to remember that spontaneous energetic movement is a totally natural part of the internal arts and is certainly nothing special. There are no links to god here and there is nothing religious about what is taking place.

I have been involved with several groups who practised some form of spontaneous energetic movement. In each case the impression was given that they were the only group who taught the technique and that the teacher of that group was the only person privy to the secret teachings of the ancients. In each case this was clearly not true. The truth is that evidence of spontaneous energetic movement can be seen through numerous spiritual traditions throughout history including the ancient Chinese, the Indian Yogis, European Shamanic circles and the Native Americans to name just a few. I recently taught a residential course in Nei Gong in Southern Sweden; one older lady informed me that the ancient Swedish also had a similar technique for keeping warm when they were out hunting in the snow of Northern Sweden but nothing remains of it apart from stories. More and more I am discovering that these practices were common knowledge in the not too distant past.

These movements are a sign that the physical and energetic bodies are coming together and that the efficiency of the meridian system is improving. Blockages are removed from the body by the movements and the health and vitality of the practitioner improves dramatically over a short period of time.

It is important to remember during the practice of spontaneous energetic movement that it is not a desired result in itself. It is simply a part of the process which should be moved through in due course. Do not revel in the movements as this will cause your mind to attach to them. At the same time, do not fight against them as this will prevent them from carrying out their work. As a guideline the movements generally seem to last somewhere between three months and a couple of years. They tend to be stronger in younger students who are closer to their teen years. This is largely due to the large degree of emotional upheaval which comes with being a teenager.

Be warned that spontaneous energetic movement can at times be quite vigorous and so there is an element of risk if you are practising in a small space with lots of furniture. Ensure that you have a lot of room around you to move in. I would also suggest that you do not practise in the company of people who do not study Nei Gong as they will think you are mad!

The spontaneous energetic movements are quite varied but generally fall into one of several categories depending on which part of the energy system is being affected. As Qi moves through the various meridians it causes the surrounding nerves to be affected which makes the body move. This is incredibly good for both the physical and energy bodies. If movements begin to take place within your body you can take your mind away from the lower Dan Tien. The work will now continue on its own for a short time and then gradually subside when it is best to take a rest for at least an hour before you continue with your practice.

Figure 6.9 shows one of my students experiencing spontaneous energetic movement.

Figure 6.9 Spontaneous Energetic Movement

CLASSIFICATION OF THE SPONTANEOUS ENERGETIC MOVEMENTS

The movements generated in a practitioner's body will vary according to which elemental energy is being affected.

Fire elemental Qi moves through four meridians which run through your arms. It is an expansive energy which causes your arms to move in an erratic manner. The movement of Fire elemental Qi can also cause energy to begin rising up through the body which can lift a person up from inside their body which results in them being uprooted; they often bounce up and down on the spot or spontaneously lift their face up towards the ceiling.

Earth elemental energy runs mainly through two long meridians which stretch the length of your body. They pass through the torso which is usually where the spontaneous energetic movements are manifested. The body begins to twist at the centre or sometimes it can dramatically spin around on the spot.

Metal elemental energy is circulated mainly through the arms but also affects the centre of the body. This energy can cause a person to contract and fold in half at their centre. It is quite common for a person to fold forwards and lose their balance which ends up with them being unceremoniously toppled onto the floor. Often, practitioners are folded in half and left hugging their knees for quite some time as the Metal Qi begins to rebalance.

Water elemental energy runs through the length of the body, both on your front and back. Spontaneous energetic movement caused by the Water elemental energy manifests as an increase in weight for the practitioner. This is not a physical increase in weight but rather a stronger connection being established with the floor. They may be pulled down towards the ground as their knees give out and often end up laid out face down on the ground. Note that this is similar in outside appearance to the movement which may be produced by 'Sung breathing' as detailed in Chapter 2 but the cause for the two movements are different.

Wood elemental energy circulates through the length of the body. Its spontaneous energetic movement is usually manifested in the legs and a practitioner begins to walk or run forward around the room uncontrollably. Sometimes the rotation of the lower Dan Tien will also cause them to spin a little and they will end up running in a large circle around the training space although this is less common.

There are also other movements which can take place which don't fall into these categories but they are fairly rare. In each case they are a manifestation of energetic movement of some sort and nothing to worry about. The movements have a positive effect on your physical health, energetic well-being and emotional state provided you approach them with the right attitude. As we have already stated, do not fight them or revel in them. If you attach your mind to the movements and see them as an important attainment you will never move past them and your development will be halted. You will have been distracted by one of the many side branches of the true path; this was a major concern of the Daoists. At the same time, enjoy the movements and experience them with an open heart. They are a funny and natural part of the process which deserves to be approached with a certain degree of good humour.

The movements should always subside on their own. You can help them to stop by lying on your back or sitting down but occasionally they will continue longer than you wish. If this is the case then simply close your eyes and calm yourself down with some deep 'Sung breathing'. Tell yourself to quieten down and then when you are completely still, go for a brisk walk outside and gently stretch the body. Next time you practise, use a much more gentle degree of focus when rotating the lower Dan Tien.

Figure 6.10 Taiwanese Spontaneous Energetic Movement

You should continue to work with the lower Dan Tien until you are happy that it is spinning freely and comfortably. From here you may begin to rotate it horizontally in either direction. The process for achieving this is exactly the same as for forward rotation. Keep the movement slow and time it with your breathing. The direction of the Dan Tien will drive Qi in different directions.

Ensure that you only practise these directions of rotation. The lower Dan Tien can turn in any direction at all but it will learn to do this on its own. Some of the other rotations carry small but nonetheless real risks if they are forced. There will naturally come a point where you feel that the Dan Tien is spinning freely within your body like an internal gyroscope. By this time your spontaneous energetic movements will have ended and you will have returned to a state of stillness in your training other than a low vibration in the lower abdomen. It is now time to move on to working directly with your Qi.

CHAPTER 7

GOING DEEPER INTO NEI GONG

Qi is primarily directed around the body by the movement of your breath and the lower Dan Tien. It is also affected by the movement of your limbs. As you open, close and rotate the various joints of your body, the movement of Qi is increased. This is because of the energy gates which sit in the joints; these important areas of the meridians system work like energetic pumps throughout the course of your daily life. The efficiency of this Qi movement is increased during practice of Qi Gong exercises.

A more advanced way to circulate Qi is to bypass the external movement altogether and direct the flow of internal energy using your mind. This is an advanced technique that requires a great deal of practice and preparatory work. This skill goes above and beyond the normal level of ability which can be gained from standard Qi Gong practice alone.

In this chapter we will look at the two stages of 'moving the Yang Qi' and the 'attainment of internal vibration'. These two skills are quite advanced; they have numerous benefits including giving the practitioner the superior health and longevity for which Daoism is well known.

Prior to working on this stage in your training you should ensure that you have built a solid foundation in the previous stages. Your body should be loose and well aligned. You should have achieved a high level of physical and mental relaxation and your joints should be free and mobile. All of this will mean that the Yang Qi can pass freely through your body.

MOVEMENT OF THE YANG QI

Once your Dan Tien is rotating smoothly and any spontaneous energetic movements have subsided you will have reached a stage whereby your energy system is fully awakened. Qi is circulated smoothly around the body which will improve the health of your organs and tissues. This energy which is led to the organs is known as the Yin Qi. Yin Qi is the Qi which is created from the Jing and then sent to the centre of your body where it nourishes the five Zang and six Fu organs. It is not necessary to understand what the difference between these two organ categories is if you do not practise Chinese medicine. It is enough to know that the body has been nourished with healthy energy.

The various meridians should be functioning efficiently and in particular the acquired or organ meridians should be relatively free of blockages. It is likely that you will already have noticed various changes taking place in your personality and outlook on life. As the health of the organs improves, so should your emotional state and you should be feeling fairly fresh and relaxed within yourself. If this is the case then the foundation has been laid for the movement of the second category of Qi: the Yang Qi.

Yang Qi is in fact exactly the same substance as the Yin Qi. The difference is to do with the area of your body which it moves to.

The Yang Qi moves out away from the centre of your body and begins to fill the various meridians which circulate the three Dan Tien. These are the following congenital meridians: the governing meridian, the conception meridian, the girdling meridian and the side branches of the thrusting meridian. The Yang Qi reaching these meridians heralds the opening of the 'small water wheels of Qi'. The Qi circulates within these meridians which form a sort of energetic cage around the three Dan Tien as shown in Figure 7.1.

Of course Qi is always circulating in these meridians to a certain degree but as with our earlier work we are aiming to increase the efficiency of the Qi circulation here so that we may reap the benefits.

The methodology for moving the Yang Qi is incredibly simple and yet at the same time very difficult. We do nothing at all. The catalyst for energetic change has been set in place by our work with the lower

Dan Tien; the manifestation of Taiji force has been awakened and so now the process of internal change has been set in motion. Instead of trying to force more results, we simply have to be patient and look for the various signs and indications of healthy progress.

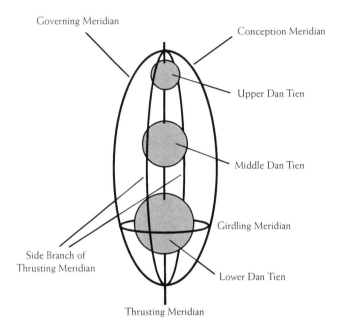

Figure 7.1 The Energetic Cage of the Small Water Wheels of Qi

The Yang Qi begins to move out and circulate within the meridians in the following order:

- First, it circulates within the governing and conception meridians. This is the first 'small water wheel of Qi' to awaken and the circulation which most Qi Gong text books refer to when they talk about the Xiao Zhou Tian or 'micro-cosmic orbit'.

- The second flow of Yang Qi circulates around the girdling meridian. This is the second 'small water wheel of Qi'.

- The third circulation takes place around the side branches of the thrusting meridian. This is the third and final 'small circulation of Qi'.

- Next the Yang Qi begins to move out towards the limbs. It circulates through the arms and legs. The meridians in the four limbs that Yang Qi moves through are branches of the thrusting meridian. Some text books refer to this as the 'macro-cosmic orbit' but according to Daoist spiritual traditions the movement of Qi here is still part of the earlier stage of awakening the 'small water wheels'.

- Finally the Yang Qi begins to move around the body in spirals. It moves out from the girdling meridian in two branches that enwrap the body. This serves to circulate Yang Qi across the surface of the skin from the top of your head down to the base of your feet.

Continue your practice of Nei Gong moving and stationary exercises daily for some time. There is no need to focus on the lower Dan Tien anymore. If you keep your awareness here it will actually slow your progress as the Yang Qi will follow the line of your intention and so be led inwards towards your lower abdomen. This is the opposite direction from where we wish it to go. At the same time, ensure that you do not try to use your mind to lead the Qi around the various 'small water wheels'. There are a great many schools that advocate the use of the mind to lead Qi around the meridians of the body but they will only achieve superficial results. The Qi must form a natural path of its own accord for the results to become permanent and integrated into your system; allow the natural rotation of the lower Dan Tien to do the work for you.

> 'The sage initiates his self-cultivation,
>
> But then lets Heaven and Earth guide him to Dao.'

The circulation of Yang Qi around the body can take several months of dedicated training. It is not unusual for a practitioner to spend several hours each day working on their Nei Gong during this period of time whilst the Yang Qi circulates. It takes patience and perseverance. Beginners reading this passage might balk at how much training is required for this stage but to be honest it is not a problem. By the time you have reached this stage, your practice will have become an extremely important part of your life. There will be no need to force the training since it will feel so natural. Your mind will become lost in your daily training and so you will lose track of time; it is very easy to while away a couple of hours without noticing it when you get to this stage. It is now that many practitioners realise that they have to make some fairly major life adjustments in order to have the necessary time for practice.

A simple set of exercises like the Ji Ben Qi Gong are ideal for this stage in your practice as they are simple enough that they don't need too much conscious thought but at the same time they work the entire body. Taiji is another useful tool to help the circulation of the Yang Qi. The Wu and Yang styles of Taiji are particularly good as they work very much on natural body movements.

Whatever you are doing, simply try to quieten the mind so that it does not get too involved in the process taking place. Follow your breathing if this helps to keep it still or simply allow it to trace over the body observing what is taking place; just ensure that it only observes and does not interfere.

The First Small Water Wheel of Qi

Your Yang Qi will initially move into the two meridians which run up your back and down your front: the governing and conception meridians. Together these two meridians make up the energetic circuit shown in Figure 7.2.

Yang Qi will initially enter the area around the base of your spine and then move up your back until it reaches the crown of your head. From here it will gradually move down the front of your body until it reaches the perineum; this is the completion of the first 'small water wheel of Qi'. The feeling of Yang Qi circulating within these two meridians should now remain with you during your regular training; unless of course you take a long break from your daily training or you suffer some kind of injury.

Yang Qi moving through these two meridians has a very distinctive feeling. It is as though you have suddenly been inflated by a bicycle pump. The Yang Qi will gradually push its way through the meridian which feels as though it has expanded to roughly the thickness of a hose pipe. It will seem as though warm air runs up the length of your back; the feeling is the same for the front of your body although in my experience it is far more subtle. Your whole torso will become incredibly loose and flexible; when you move it will look as though your entire body ripples from deep within its core. This is a sign that your external body has linked in to the movement of your lower Dan Tien and an excellent sign of progress. If you watch a person with a strong circulation of Qi in these meridians they will look as though they are made of fluid when they perform their Qi Gong exercises; it is particularly clear to see if they also practise some form of internal martial art such as Taiji.

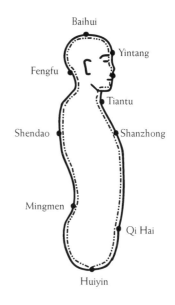

Figure 7.2 The First Small Water Wheel of Qi

If you previously had any kind of muscular-skeletal injury to your spine or torso, it should no longer be apparent to you. I personally smashed the bones in my left shoulder and collar bone in an accident during martial arts training when I was younger. The injury severely weakened my left side and left me with a lot of pain and tightness which extended into the muscles around the top of my spine and neck. Once the Yang Qi circulated through my governing and conception meridians the pain faded away and the strength returned to my left side.

PROBLEM SHOOTING IN THE FIRST SMALL WATER WHEEL

It is quite common for people to start to experience Yang Qi flowing into the governing meridian only to find that it 'gets stuck' in one of several points. The point at which your Yang Qi is stuck will feel slightly uncomfortable; it is as though you have a deep bruise in this area of your body. You will also find that your flexibility will be greatly reduced in this area as the muscles tighten up. Figure 7.2 shows the various points where the Yang Qi might get stuck. These points are as follows: Mingmen (GV4), Shendao (GV11), Fengfu (GV16), Baihui (GV20), Yintang (Extra 2), Huiyin (CV1), Qi Hai (CV6), Shanzhong (CV17) and Tiantu (CV22).

The Yang Qi may get stuck in one of the above points due to any slight misalignment. This is particularly true of the points in your back or on the front of your torso. It may also be due to an energetic blockage in this area. Once you have checked your alignments and ascertained that the problem is due to a blockage simply return to the 'Sung breathing' process and release the blockage in this area. Stick with this process until you feel the Yang Qi begin to move past this point.

In the majority of cases, when you first get to this stage in your training, Mingmen will take some time to align and open up. It is particularly important to get the Yang Qi to circulate past this point due to Mingmen's relationship with your lower Dan Tien and the kidneys. Be very thorough when working with this point and ensure that the Yang Qi circulates well through this area of your back before you try to progress onto the other points.

THE SECOND SMALL WATER WHEEL OF QI

Only once the Yang Qi circulates through your governing and conception meridians will it begin to move into the girdling meridian. The girdling meridian runs around your waist and the lower Dan Tien area as we have already discussed in Chapter 2.

As Yang Qi moves into the girdling meridian you will experience the same 'inflated' feeling that you should already have in your torso. The movements of your lower Dan Tien should tie very strongly into the physical area of your waist leaving you with a very strong sense of 'centre'. This is evident when you perform any twisting motion in your practice; it will feel as though the movement of your entire body is generated from the area of the lower Dan Tien. This does not necessarily require a strong external turn of the waist; the movement will feel as though it is generated from deep within your core. This is a sign of an energetic connection being developed between the lower and upper halves of your body.

THE THIRD SMALL WATER WHEEL OF QI

The feeling of Yang Qi moving within the side branches of the thrusting meridian is a little more subtle than the previous two sensations. The feeling is almost as if your insides are melting. You will find that you feel as if there is a great deal of fluid moving around inside your torso that leaves you feeling incredibly soft on the inside but at the same time very strong and physically connected. It becomes much easier to open and close the various joints of the body during Nei Gong practice; you will even be able to feel the rib cage opening and closing with your movements.

One of the most difficult areas of the physical body to open up is the area known as the shoulders nest in Daoism. Figure 7.3 shows the shoulders nest area.

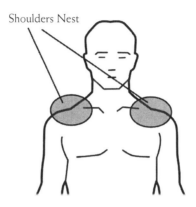

Figure 7.3 The Shoulders Nest

Once Yang Qi moves within the two side branches of the thrusting meridian you will feel the shoulders nest areas begin to open up as though they had been inflated from within you. This produces a feeling as though you are thrusting out the chest but an outside observer will not be able to see any change in your posture. If the shoulders nest areas are not sufficiently open you will not be able to circulate Yang Qi into the arms.

YANG QI MOVES INTO THE LIMBS

You have now managed to attain the three main 'small water wheels of Qi'. The next stage is the circulation of Qi through the arms and legs.

In some texts the movement of Yang Qi out into the limbs is known as the 'large water wheel of Qi' or the 'macro-cosmic orbit'. For various reasons terminology can differ across Daoist sects and a term like this can mean several different things. In this book we talk about the circulation of Yang Qi through the limbs as another stage in the 'small water wheel of Qi'. This is because the Qi is still being circulated within the microcosm of your own body; the 'large water wheel of Qi' instead refers to the circulation of energy and information out of your body into the macrocosm of the surrounding environment. This is not to say that the aforementioned classical texts are incorrect; it is simply a different use of terminology.

Yang Qi moving out into your arms and hands is a natural process which will begin to happen of its own accord. There is no need to use a strong mental intention to lead the Qi out of your hands. Instead, carry on with your regular practice and allow your mind to follow the process of internal change which is unfolding within you.

Your arms will begin to feel very light and at times it is almost as though you have no arms at all. This feeling will last for some time before you will experience the same 'inflated' sensation that moved through your body in the previous stages. It is a remarkable stage when your arms feel as though they are filled with helium! They will even begin to move of their own accord sometimes during Qi Gong practice and 'float' up into the air when you are lifting your arms.

Despite feeling light and full of air, your physical strength should increase dramatically. This was particularly difficult for me as a martial artist. Due to no longer feeling my muscles engage when I moved my arms I believed myself to be weakening. I felt frail as though I were made of paper. When engaging in partner practice I found that the opposite was true; I was now able to lift and throw my partners with hardly any effort at all. As long as I remained relaxed and kept the same principles of movement within my partner training I was far stronger than most people, no matter if they were much larger than me.

When observing the movements of somebody with Yang Qi circulating through the arms you will see that they almost seem to have no shoulders, elbows or wrists. Their arms look more like tentacles that undulate and flow in a soft and yet powerful manner.

It is a much longer process to move Yang Qi down into the legs as they tend to be more tense than the arms. It is not unusual for there to be a gap of several months between the Yang Qi moving into the arms and the legs.

When the legs become filled with Yang Qi they become very loose and light. The joints around your hips and knees become very flexible and mobile as if they had just been freshly oiled. It is only at this stage that you realise just how tense your lower body has been in comparison to your upper body throughout your training. Although your legs feel light, you will be much more 'rooted' to the floor when you practise standing Qi Gong exercises. It will also feel as though your upper body weighs nothing whatsoever; your legs no longer have any pressure bearing down on them from above which means that they can move in an incredibly free and loose manner. You will experience a freedom of movement which you have not had since being a young child.

CIRCULATING THE YANG QI ACROSS THE SKIN

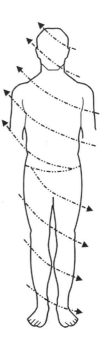

The final movements of Yang Qi begin in the area of the lower Dan Tien and the girdling meridian. You will begin to experience a strong spiralling movement which expands out from your lower abdomen and enwraps your body. Two branches move out from your centre towards the crown of your head and the base of your feet. Figure 7.4 shows the direction of this flow of Yang Qi.

You will feel the flow of energy moving out across the surface of your skin. This is a fairly brief stage of development; I personally only experienced it for a period of a few days. This is a sign of your Yang Qi permeating the skin and Wei Qi field which we discussed in Chapter 2.

This is the final circulation of Yang Qi within the microcosm of the body; it indicates that you are ready to move on with your Nei Gong training.

Figure 7.4 Spiralling Yang Qi

THE REJUVENATING EFFECT OF YANG QI

Yang Qi circulating through the body has several physical effects which can be seen. Use these physical changes as indications of progress in your training. Whilst cosmetic changes are not really that important in the grand scheme of Daoism, they are useful indications of our practice heading in the right direction.

- Your face becomes very smooth and develops a slightly 'moist' look to it. It is almost as if your face were slightly greasy yet at the same time it does not look dirty. It almost looks as if you were wearing moisturiser.

- Your eyes become very sharp and piercing with a bright shine to them. A skilled internal arts practitioner can tell a great deal about your stage of development by the nature of your eyes. The Chinese would say that your Shen shines through your eyes whilst in the West we would say that they are the 'window to your soul'.

- The skin all over your body suddenly becomes quite loose and rubbery. This is due to the layers of fascia unbinding as the Qi permeates through your body. It is possible to stretch your skin to quite a degree. Often, the majority of wrinkles will disappear from your face when you attain this stage in your practice.

- Practitioners with grey hair may discover that some of it changes back to its original colour. Whilst your entire head may not go back to its former glory, patches of coloured hair will grow back as your blood and scalp are nourished by the movement of Yang Qi.

- Your entire physical body should become very loose and free. A practitioner who has attained this stage should look very fluid and smooth when they move. There should be no signs of stiffness or tension in their movements. It is important to note that flexibility and looseness are entirely different things. A person can be very flexible with regard to how far they may bend their body but they may still be tense. A person who practises Nei Gong to a high standard should be very loose and free within their range of bodily movement; that being said, they should still be fairly flexible although there is no need to be a contortionist.

SENSATION INFORMATION

The feeling of 'inflation' which comes with the movement of Yang Qi is only the body's way of experiencing the information contained within the vibrational wave which circulates through the 'small water wheels of Qi'. This is the same as any other physical sensation which you experience during the course of your life. Physical sensation is not an external entity; it is generated by your own consciousness. This is the root of the Buddhist and Daoist concept of the physical world being false.

The feeling of 'inflation' which comes with this stage in your training will be temporary. Once the mind and body become used to this new sensation it will no longer generate the feelings from the vibrational information contained within the Yang Qi. The sensations will be 'normalised' and so the feeling will begin to fade away until you feel exactly as you did before this stage in your internal development. It is a shame since the feeling of Yang Qi 'inflating' the various meridians is very pleasant. The sensations seem to last for a period which last from several months to a year before they begin to vanish. The amount of time seems to vary from person to person. You will, however, be left with the physical signs which we listed above and your physical movements will retain the qualities we have already discussed.

Some students worry when the feelings begin to fade away. They fear that they have made a mistake or that they are not training hard enough. This is not the case. Look for the external signs of change which we have listed above and continue until you have attained the stage of circulating the Yang Qi over the surface of your skin. It is quite likely that by the time you reach this stage, you will already have lost the 'inflated' feeling of Yang Qi moving through the governing and conception meridians.

ATTAINMENT OF INTERNAL VIBRATION
Up until now you will probably have been working mostly with moving Qi Gong exercises; perhaps the Ji Ben Qi Gong set. These movements will have given you a platform from which to begin integrating the various principles inherent within Nei Gong. If you are ready to start working at this stage then you are already an advanced practitioner of Nei Gong.

It is now time for the emphasis of your training to switch to stationary exercises. Nei Gong sits somewhere between conventional

Daoist internal exercises and the meditative practice of internal alchemy. The stage of developing a strong internal vibration sits exactly on the borderline between these two practices. This is because we have reached the stage of working directly with the subtle energies of the thrusting meridian.

The thrusting meridian is particularly important within Daoist practices. It primarily serves to transport the three substances of Jing, Qi and Shen through the body once they have been refined within the three Dan Tien. It also provides a direct line of communication between the lower and upper Dan Tien which is very important for the alchemy process when we 'invert Kan Li' as described in Chapter 6. There are also three other main functions which are not as widely discussed within contemporary internal arts texts. These are as follows:

- The thrusting meridian provides a channel for our consciousness to drop down through and link in with the rest of our energy system.

- The central branch of the thrusting meridian runs from the crown of the head to the perineum. Energetic movement along this line serves to divide the two poles within the human body which in turn leads to development of the 'large water wheel of Qi'.

- To the ancient Daoists, the central branch of the thrusting meridian served as a kind of 'spiritual antenna' which would enable an advanced practitioner to receive spiritual information from the very cosmos.

In order to experientially understand the various functions of the thrusting meridian we must first find a way to access it with our mind. We do this through development of a high frequency internal vibration which we pass through the length of the thrusting meridian's central branch. This vibration moves from the perineum up through our body until it reaches the crown; this vibration allows us to drop our mental intention down into the core of our body and so awaken some of the more esoteric aspects of our energetic system.

DEVELOPING INTERNAL VIBRATION WITHIN THE THRUSTING
MERIDIAN

For this practice we need to adopt the sitting position shown in Figure 7.5. This is the basic posture for carrying out sitting practices within Daoism.

Those with considerable experience in meditation may use the more advanced half-lotus or full-lotus positions if they wish. Whilst these positions are required for some of the later stages in internal alchemy they are not necessary for the development of internal vibration through the thrusting meridian. If you try to force yourself into the lotus position when your body is

Figure 7.5 Seated Practice

not sufficiently conditioned you will create tension which will weaken your practice and possibly even damage your hip, knee or ankle joints. Prop yourself up on a small cushion as shown in Figure 7.5. Ensure that your hips are higher than your knees. The cushion should not be so soft that you sink into it nor too hard that it is uncomfortable as this will distract you from your practice. Make sure that your spine is correctly aligned on top of your pelvis which is not collapsed forwards. You should not slump your body down in seated practice as this will close down all of the energy points on your body which you have spent so long opening up through your Nei Gong practice. The position of your legs ensures that your perineum and more importantly a point called Huiyin (CV1) is open. This is the area from which the internal vibration you are seeking originates.

Within Daoist practices there are various hand positions which serve different functions. In Chinese these are known as 'Shoujue' but they are more commonly known as Mudra (which is a Sanskrit term) within the West. It is not necessary to have an in-depth understanding of Daoism's many hand positions when you are studying Nei Gong with the exception of the Shoujue shown in Figure 7.6. We use this hand position during the exercise outlined here.

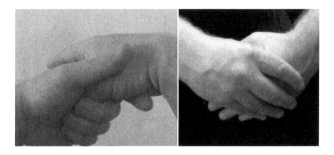

Figure 7.6 Daoist Shoujue

Practise forming the hand position from the steps shown above. Your hands should be relaxed and you should only be using a very light grip. The most important factor is that the tips of each thumb should be resting on the Laogong (PC8) point of the opposite palm. This serves a very important purpose. Laogong is an important point for venting excess heat from the body. Within this exercise we wish to keep the inside of our body relatively warm as this heat provides an external catalyst for the process taking place. The above hand position stops this heat from escaping; consequently sweat will begin to pour out of your palms after only a few minutes of the following exercise. This is nothing to worry about.

Begin to practise your 'Sung breathing'. It is likely that you will already be able to nourish the body with the energetic frequencies of Heaven and Earth as described in Chapter 3. If so, allow these two forces to move through the body. They will help to open up the energy gates and free the meridian system up which will make the movement of the internal vibration through the thrusting meridian easier to attain. If you have built a solid enough foundation in the previous stages you should not develop any discomfort from sitting for a prolonged period of time. Your legs should not go to sleep and your back should not hurt. This is important as this exercise requires you to have the ability to sit for at least an hour to 90 minutes comfortably.

Once you are sure that your body is sufficiently prepared and you are relaxed and comfortable we will begin to try and unite our energy body with the outside environment.

Bring your awareness to rest lightly on the area of the perineum. Ensure that you do not use an overly strong intention; you should be very comfortable with using the correct intensity of focus by now. This area can easily be found by dropping your mind straight down from the lower Dan Tien until it reaches the limit of your physical body. Keep your awareness on this point for a few minutes and you will soon feel the warmth of the Jing in this area of your body being slightly stirred. We are not aiming to work with the Jing but this is a sign that our consciousness is functioning at the correct frequency for our practice.

For the next stage, allow your awareness to gently expand up the length of the central branch of the thrusting meridian until it reaches the crown of the head. Progress slowly and steadily until you have managed to extend your focus from the Huiyin (CV1) point to Baihui (GV20). It is vitally important that you do not try to use your mind to lead Qi to this area. This will run the risk of creating Qi deviation as Yang Qi is led from the outside of your body towards the core. You will know if this is happening as you will begin to experience spontaneous energetic movements which contort your body and cause the spine to undulate as it did in earlier stages of your practice. If this happens, start your practice again with a far gentler awareness. Remember that you should keep in mind the idea of 'casually observing' everything that is taking place. Note that it is very easy to make this mistake when working on this exercise. Do not worry if spontaneous energetic movement like this occurs; you would have to continue practising in this incorrect fashion for a prolonged period of time for problems to occur.

Once you have the correct level of awareness extended along the length of the thrusting meridian you should simply sit and wait. Keep your mind quiet and be patient. After a short time, usually about an hour or so, you will begin to feel the energies of the thrusting meridian begin to awaken. This will feel like a deep vibrating wave which starts at the perineum and then surges up towards the crown like a wave. Figure 7.7 shows the direction of travel of this wave.

As the wave moves through your body it is accompanied by a feeling of euphoria which overtakes the whole body. You will begin to shake deep within your core as the energy of the

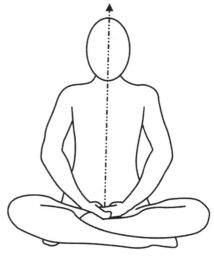

Figure 7.7 Vibration along the Thrusting Meridian

spine begins to integrate with your physical and energetic bodies. This internal shaking is very different from the spontaneous movements discussed in Chapter 6; they are far deeper within the body and much smaller. You will become aware of the shaking opening your body up from within and it will seem as though your hips are moving down into the floor whilst the crown of your head is lifted up into the sky.

ADDICTION TO THE INTERNAL VIBRATION

There is one major risk attached to this level of attainment: addiction to the sensation. Human beings experience this feeling throughout the course of their lives when they have sex, particularly with a person they feel deeply in love with. During orgasm, the central branch of the thrusting meridian opens up to allow this internal vibration to move through the body. It is more common for women to experience orgasm throughout the whole of their body provided that there is an emotional attachment to their partner. The deep emotions help to lead the vibration up through the thrusting meridian and then out into the physical body. Men may also experience this feeling although it is rarer due to the ejaculation which usually accompanies their orgasm. Ejaculation restricts the feeling of internal vibration to the genital area and does not allow it to move through the body. If men are able to separate ejaculation from orgasm then they too will experience the whole body orgasm of the thrusting meridian vibrating. These sensations are very much attached to our physical desires and so they can become very addictive. There is a danger of people reaching this stage in their training and becoming too attached to the feeling of the vibration moving through their spine, particularly men who may not find it so easy to experience the whole body euphoria which comes from this practice. If your mind attaches to this sensation then you will never move past it and so your progress will be halted. You need to demonstrate great resolve in your training; acknowledge the process taking place and then 'casually observe' what is taking place as before.

Internal vibration of this kind also brings about a great increase in sexual desire. The body will develop a great deal more sexual fluid and your sexual organs will also increase in size and sensitivity. This is only a temporary change and once you move on you will find that your sexual organs have returned to their previous state. You will also find that you will be more attractive to the opposite sex whose energy bodies will subconsciously read the information from your thrusting meridian. These are all temptations which must be ignored. In the past a great many Daoist practitioners did not manage to resist the temptations here and so were led down the wrong path. Many deviant sexual practices were developed including group sex and methods for draining the Jing of virgin girls. Whole sects of Daoism went down this path in the misguided belief that they could use sex to attain spiritual elevation. This is simply not the case. If enlightenment could be reached through sex it would be a far more attractive life choice to the majority of people!

DIVISION OF THE TWO POLES

If you manage to resist the temptations attached to this stage in your practice and keep your mind still you will soon begin to separate the 'two poles' within your body. Once the wave of euphoria and vibration has started, it should only take a few weeks of daily practice to move past this into the division of the two poles. Work through this exercise in the mornings, mid-day and evenings whilst keeping the rest of your day as simple as possible to ensure swift progress. It may be best to retreat from the rest of your life for a period of a few weeks at this stage in your practice; the simpler your life is and the less distractions the better during this period.

> 'Existence supports Yin and embraces Yang,
>
> They exist together through the power of Qi,
>
> If we can harness the Qi then we can understand the poles of Yin and Yang.'

The two poles are the extremes of Yin and Yang within your body; they are similar to the positive and negative poles of a magnet. The poles sit at the area of Baihui (GV20) and Huiyin (CV1). As the two poles begin to form you will feel these two areas begin to spiral and pull apart into the sky and down into the floor. Remember that they are not really moving at all. The Qi within this part of the body is stirring which causes it to vibrate more; this vibration carries information as we have already discussed. The mind translates this information as a physical sensation which feels like the two poles are spiralling. At this stage the feelings of euphoria will have subsided and the vibration within your thrusting meridian will have become far more subtle, so it no longer causes you to physically shake.

THE LARGE WATER WHEEL OF QI

Once the two poles have formed, your energy system will be able to effectively communicate with the macrocosm of the environment around you. Qi and Shen will be able to circulate through the length of the central branch of the thrusting meridian and out of the body via Baihui and Huiyin. It will form the circuit shown in Figure 7.8. This is similar to the fields which surround a magnet.

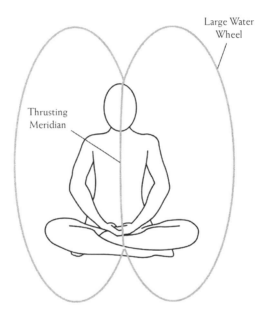

Figure 7.8 Large Water Wheel

This circulation is known as the 'large water wheel of Qi' or the 'macrocosmic orbit' since the energy circulates out of the microcosm of your body into the macrocosm of the surrounding environment.

It is a combination of both Qi and Shen which moves through the circuit of the 'large water wheel of Qi'. This means that our consciousness interacts with both our physical surroundings and our own body to a far higher degree than before. This is particularly important for practitioners of Nei Gong for a variety of reasons. First, you will find that your mind is far more in touch with your physical body than before. You will begin to become aware of the state of each and every organ within the body; you will instinctively know when imbalance and illness are beginning to occur within you. Your taste in food will change as you subconsciously know what food is best for your body. If you begin to feel ill you will often feel the blockage starting to appear within your body and with a mental intent you can push this blockage from the body; there is no longer any need for the 'Sung breathing' technique. It is also common for practitioners to begin to gravitate towards certain times of the day and even wish to face different directions when they practise depending upon what your energy system needs at that particular time.

The Shen circulating outside of your body through the circuits shown in Figure 7.8 begins to make you more in tune with your environment. You will begin to develop an awareness of the Qi around you and the information contained within it. You will be able to tell the emotional state of people around you and at the same time your own state of being will begin to affect those with whom you come into contact. You will not have reached this stage in your training unless your mind is fairly settled and you are relatively calm and still inside. Others will find that they are drawn towards you and that they feel calmer when they are around you. Anybody who has spent time around an advanced practitioner of Qi Gong or meditation will be familiar with the calming energy which surrounds them. There are of course risks attached to this stage. The attainment of the 'large water wheel of Qi' means that people will naturally gravitate towards you and look up to you. In a world where many people live in a constant state of turmoil, they will look to you for answers. It is vitally important to remember that you are not an enlightened being just yet! You will still be subject to the perversions of your own Ego and so must remain as humble as you can. Do not allow the fact that people look to you for guidance distort your nature or else you may end up taking advantage of people. Nei Gong practice can bring great amounts of power to a person who is willing to use it for their own ends. I have met teachers who have had this happen to them and also experienced myself the pull of the Ego that came with this level of attainment. For a time I found myself thriving on the way others looked to me for guidance; the feeling of power and self-importance is easily as addictive as the euphoria and whole body orgasm attached to the attainment of internal vibration. It was only after a period of self-imposed isolation and contemplation that I managed to avoid the temptations of the Ego. On a purely selfish level, if you go down this route you will halt your progress; the Daoists knew that this was the universal law of the internal arts.

COMMUNICATION BETWEEN YOUR MIND AND BODY

When the 'large water wheel of Qi' has been achieved you will be circulating a certain amount of Shen, the energy of consciousness through both your energy system and your physical body. This causes a fascinating change to take place in the way your body works. As a practitioner of the martial arts I spend a great deal of time studying body movements and so for me this was a particularly profound development in my training. The linking of your mind to your body means that you are now able to direct your movements with just a thought.

Start to practise this skill by carrying out a very simple movement such as raising and lowering one arm. Start with your arm resting loosely at your side. Now using only mental intention begin the movement. Do not assist your arm in any way by engaging your muscles; you should use nothing but mental intent.

If you have successfully opened the 'large water wheel of Qi' you will find that your arm will easily follow your mental intention. The sensation is subtly different from how you may have moved before as the muscles hardly do any work at all and so no excess tension is created. It is only now that you can appreciate how inefficiently you have been using your body up until this time. You have spent years wasting a great deal of effort and utilising muscles that were not really needed. Movements generated from your mind are very relaxed and soft with no tension. This will result in a greater degree of movement within your bodily joints and a dramatic rise in your flexibility as your body is literally not working against you as it probably has been in the past.

Practise different body movements. You will find that you are able to completely control everything you do using just mental intention. Martial artists will reach new heights of skill and discover that their stamina will increase tenfold as they no longer waste energy when they move. Wasted muscular contraction will no longer be a problem and so the speed of your strikes will increase along with your reaction speed as the previous 'lag time' that existed between your mind and body disappears. Attaining the 'large water wheel of Qi' is the key to becoming an expert in the martial arts and the way to ensure that your skill increases as you age. Your muscles may grow weaker as you get older but your Shen can increase provided you train correctly; harness your Shen and martial artists will beat the ageing process which ruins many martial artists' training.

THE THRUSTING MERIDIAN AS A SPIRITUAL ANTENNA

The Daoists believed that a fully open and functioning thrusting meridian acted as a sort of spiritual antenna that enabled you to draw various layers of spiritual information from the very cosmos. They called this phenomenon the 'magical knowing' and some sects spent a great deal of information aiming to develop this skill. It was believed that a person would be able to rise above time and space and so in some cases gain cosmic information on the past and future. It was also believed that you would be able to draw teachings from the spirits of long-dead masters who had attained spiritual immortality. These ancient lineages would share their wisdom with those able to communicate on a spiritual level with the realm of pure consciousness.

I do not wish to spend time looking in detail at this function of the thrusting meridian as information is very scarce. I have had my own experiences with this area of Nei Gong training as well as training under teachers who were able to demonstrate various aspects of this skill. However, I do not really understand the process involved here and it seems to be a naturally unfolding process after the 'large water wheel of Qi' has begun. Rather than run the risk of giving incorrect and false information based purely upon my own speculation I will allow other practitioners of Nei Gong to experience this stage for themselves. I do not believe that an unenlightened being such as myself could fathom the nature of the realm of pure consciousness.

Box 7.1 Nei Gong and Chinese Medicine

One of the main branches of Daoism is Chinese medicine. Acupuncture is as widespread as arts like Taiji and Qi Gong here in the West and every day many people turn to Chinese medicine when the conventional healthcare system has failed them.

Traditionally Qi Gong was taught alongside Chinese medicine although in modern times this practice is less common. Many contemporary schools of Chinese medicine either completely ignore this aspect of the training or pay lip service to it with only a very small amount of internal training. This is a real shame since the effectiveness of acupuncture is greatly increased if the practitioner has reached a fairly high degree of internal development. Qi Gong alone will help a therapist to extend their Qi into the patient but if the Qi Gong is used to work through the various stages of Nei Gong then this effectiveness is increased again.

The treatment should begin from the second a patient walks into the therapist's room. A skilled therapist who has worked heavily on their own energy system should be able to use the information transmission to their advantage. When diagnosing they will be able to use their intuition to a far higher level. They may be able to draw information directly from their patient's energetic field which is invaluable when deciding on a course of treatment. During the treatment the therapist should train to expand their energy field to encompass their patient. With the correct level of intention this energetic field should surround the patient and begin to dredge through their system before the needles are even put into their body.

The benefit of Qi Gong exercises can also be carried over into the patient. Qi Gong exercises work to balance and regulate the energy of the Jing Luo. A skilled Chinese medicine practitioner could prescribe a particular prescription of Qi Gong exercises which would enhance the healing effect of a therapy such as acupuncture or massage. This is already a common practice in more traditional Chinese medicine centres in the East.

In short, practices such as Qi Gong and Nei Gong are an integral part of Chinese medicine and should not be ignored by any sincere practitioner.

CHAPTER 8

ADVANCED NEI GONG PRACTICE

The earlier stages of Nei Gong training work primarily with our Jing and Qi. It is at the later stages in our Nei Gong practice that we begin to work directly with our Shen. Shen vibrates at a much higher frequency than our Jing or Qi and so is furthest from the physical realm. It is the energy of consciousness, thought and intention. All of the work up until this point has been solely to build a strong foundation for the conversion of Qi to Shen which is the key to accessing the various parts of the human consciousness. In order to understand this stage in their development, the ancient Daoists used a conceptual framework known as the theory of Heart-Mind. At this stage in your training you are beginning to move into the realm of meditation.

> 'Spiritual energy: your Shen
>
> Resides in the spiritual valley – the hidden source of existence.
>
> The spiritual valley is the mysterious pass from which Heaven and Earth are born.'

What is commonly known as Daoist meditation can be divided into three broad categories: visualisation, contemplation and transformation. Understanding the difference between these three types of meditation can help you to understand the aims of the meditation.

VISUALISATION

The first category of meditation uses a great deal of imagery. A practitioner will usually conjure up a specific image within their mind's eye. This can be a single image or a series of images which leads the mind through a particular process. These images can be directed inwards, for example, some Daoist methods involve picturing flames and lights moving through the body. External imagery can also be used such as external lights shining down onto the practitioner. In rare cases, Daoist deities are pictured hovering around the practitioner although this is not in line with the original teachings of the *Dao De Jing*.

Visualisation meditation can vary greatly in effectiveness. The benefits can vary from improvements in health and internal sensitivity through to drastic changes in a practitioner's mindset. The danger is that imagination takes over and a person can become deluded into thinking that they have achieved something that they haven't. In order to avoid this happening, ensure that the external signs of progress we have discussed within this book are evident within your body.

Daoists know this method as being a lesser method and whilst it may have certain uses for beginners, it is unlikely that a person will attain the higher stages with this method alone.

CONTEMPLATION

Contemplation involves allowing the mind to focus entirely on an ideal or concept. Within traditional schools of Daoism it was the norm to spend great deals of time studying the ancient scriptures and philosophies of Dao. A student needed to understand such arcane texts as the *Dao De Jing* and *I Ching*. The nature of these texts is very complex and a student was required to study each passage in depth before remaining in quiet contemplation until the concept had soaked into their very psyche. In this way the teachings of Daoism began to change the way that a student's mind worked and how he or she perceived the world.

In modern times contemplation of this kind is rarely emphasised. The philosophy of Daoism is secondary in importance to the practices.

TRANSFORMATION

The third main category of Daoist meditation is the way of transformation. The early stages concern converting Jing to Qi to Shen through focusing the mind on different areas of the body such as the various meridian points and the three Dan Tien. The higher stages work on altering the mind through initiating an internal change rather than visualisations or contemplating the ancient texts.

We can see that the techniques of Nei Gong are more akin to the transformative system of meditation although it also contains some visualisation and contemplation of Daoist theory. The stage of working directly with Shen which we will discuss in this chapter is solely concerned with the transformation method.

PRAYER

I feel that it is also important at this stage to mention the religious practice of prayer. Whilst prayer is not strictly speaking a form of meditation it does share some of its properties. The majority of prayer seeks some kind of external inspiration. It is usually either a way to speak directly to or to show devotion to a higher power or god. Prayer is not traditionally a part of Daoism since structured religion is frowned upon within the *Dao De Jing* but contemporary religious Daoism does sometimes include the practice of prayer.

Discussion of the similarities between meditation and religious prayer is often a controversial subject. It is not the purpose of this book to deliberately cause controversy or to offend followers of any faith but we should look in brief at how prayer affects the consciousness from the point of view of Nei Gong.

The higher stages of Nei Gong aim to work with our Shen. Through our training we build up an abundance of Shen which is then used within our practice to change the nature of our consciousness. This in turn leads to the state of being which is commonly known as enlightenment. There are distinct signs of the Shen forming and moving which we will discuss in this chapter; these signs are identical to phenomena inherent within the majority of religious practices. The Nei Gong view is that we have attained a higher state of consciousness which has enabled us to reconnect with the energy of the cosmos. Religions often see the same attainments as signs of communication with a divine power or god.

From this we can see that prayer and meditation may lead us to exactly the same place. Both religion and spiritual practice are simply conceptual frameworks which enable us to understand a complex idea.

Prayer and meditation are not mutually exclusive practices; they both provide glimpses into the ancient teachings of our ancestors.

I will allow readers to draw their own conclusion from this chapter concerning the similar results which can be gained from meditation and religious prayer.

THE FUNCTIONS OF SHEN

Our Shen carries out several functions which can be complex to understand at first. Like so much within Nei Gong it is much easier to understand experientially than intellectually. Within Chinese medicine the heart is known as the seat of our Shen. This is because our Shen is converted from our Qi within the middle Dan Tien which sits in the centre of our chest at the level of our heart. It is here that the energetic manifestation of Shen is directed out into the energy body in the form of our emotions. Our emotions serve to disperse the majority of our Shen and help form the false sense of self which we know as the Ego. Our Shen is also linked to the various aspects of what the Chinese call our spirit such as our two souls (the Hun and the Po), our will-power (Zhi) and our intellect (Yi).

We need to develop an abundance of Shen by working with these various elements so that we may direct some of it upwards into the upper Dan Tien which sits in the area of our brain. Figure 8.1 summarises the various functions of the Shen.

Our will-power or 'Zhi' is formed from a combination of our Jing and our Shen according to Daoist thought. The formative power of Jing gives a strong, almost tangible form to our thought. There are various risks attached to somebody with too much will-power as they will quickly drain their Kidney energy. It is as important for us to rest our mind as it is for us to rest our physical body.

Our intellect is related to the health of our Spleen, in particular our ability to learn and memorise information. In modern times the majority of people have some sort of Spleen deficiency which is caused by our poor diet. The Daoists recognised that imbalances of the Spleen had a direct effect on our intellect. This may be difficult for Western readers to accept as we generally restrict our definition of intellect as pertaining to our brain.

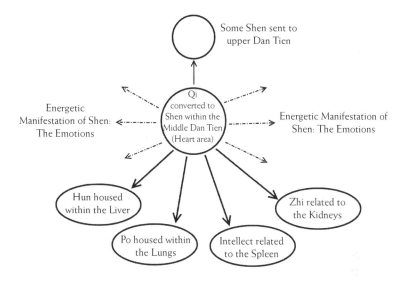

Figure 8.1 Functions of the Shen

The Po is our 'corporeal soul' in Daoist thought. We have two souls, one Yang and one Yin. The Po is our Yin soul and governs various factors of our consciousness including physical sensation. Our Po is directly linked with our physical body and dies with us whilst the Yang soul continues after our death. The Shen which is formed within the middle Dan Tien also directs the Po which is said to be housed within the Lungs. If the energy or our Lungs is out of balance then our Po is affected which in turn drains some of our Shen.

The Hun is commonly known as our 'ethereal soul'. It is Yang in nature and is most similar in concept to the soul we may talk about in Western thought since it is immortal and continues to exist after our death. Our Hun is linked to the side of our consciousness which deals with our destiny. A person with a healthy Hun will have a strong sense of purpose in life. If the Hun is weak then all sense of purpose of lost. According to Daoist thought, the Liver houses the Hun and so an imbalance of the Liver energy can detrimentally affect the Hun and so in turn the Shen. Many of us have at some point experienced the feeling of 'floating' out of our body just before going to sleep; it is almost as though the bed is tipping. This is a sign that the Hun is out of balance.

Within the area of the heart and middle Dan Tien the Shen is being formed from the Qi. This means that the Shen has its strongest influence over the energy body in this area. The heart has long been connected with the emotions in the majority of traditions throughout history; Daoism is no exception. From the area of the heart, five main energetic movements are born. The information contained within these five energies are our emotions.

OUR EMOTIONS AND THE HEART-MIND

Obviously there are more than five emotions which a person can experience and any attempt to conceptualise them will be a gross over-simplification but for the purposes of Nei Gong we generally divide the emotions into five main categories (see Table 8.1).

Table 8.1 The Emotional Manifestations of the Wu Xing

Fire	Earth	Metal	Water	Wood
Mania/Joy	Worry	Grief/Sadness	Fear/Paranoia	Anger

For more information on how the energetic imbalances affect us please refer to Chapter 2.

Before we can move any deeper into our Nei Gong training we need to be able to bring the emotions under our control. If we do not then the majority of our Shen is dispersed and so we cannot send it to the upper Dan Tien. It is important to understand that we are not trying to delete our emotions. I have had students concerned when beginning this practice that they are going to become devoid of emotions; this is really not the case. Rather than destroying our emotions we are aiming to convert them into what the Daoists called 'Te' or virtues. The five virtues are refined versions of the energetic movements which usually generate our emotions. They are qualities which would traditionally be associated with sage-like characters and an outward sign of our Ego being dissolved so that our true consciousness can shine forth.

If we look at the Heart-Mind concept (Figure 8.2) we can see how our true consciousness is buried beneath the various layers of our false sense of self.

Human beings interact primarily with the external world through their senses. We use our perceptions of touch, taste, sight, smell and hearing to interpret information from our surrounding environment. From here this information is passed into the human mind. Note that the human mind is very different from human consciousness. The human mind only processes information which is taken in; it does not generate thought or awareness. You can think of the human mind as being like a computer. A computer does not do anything that it is not programmed to do by its user. The user of the computer is human consciousness.

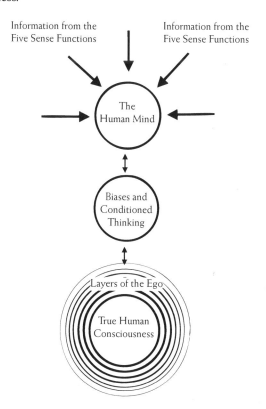

Figure 8.2 The Heart-Mind

The information which is taken into the mind is then affected by the biases and learning which we have picked up through our life. The process of developing biases begins as soon as a person is born and continues throughout the rest of their life. Some of this learning is useful, for example we quickly learn that a fire is hot and so we do not touch fire for fear of burning ourselves. Other information which we learn is not useful, for example a person has a bad experience at night once and so for the rest of their life attaches feelings of nervousness to the dark. Each of us carries with us a vast amount of information like this which is formed from past memories, associations and experiences. Along with this we may have prejudices and knowledge given to us by our family, friends, media and the education system to name just a few. It is practically impossible to generate a thought that does not have some kind of association or memory attached to it. The biases and conditioned thinking which we have picked up in this manner distort the information which we take in through our senses long before it reaches our consciousness.

This information serves to create a 'shell' around our true consciousness. We call this shell the 'false sense of self' or the Ego. The Ego is the 'fake' us which we generally associate with. Like a mask we wear the Ego throughout our life. When we were first born our true consciousness was all that we had. According to Daoist thought we were already in an enlightened state but for one problem, we lacked intelligence. We require the intellect that comes from learning and ageing in order to fulfil our innate destiny to attain enlightenment. Unfortunately the intelligence we gain through learning also brings the biases which distort our inner nature and so develop the Ego. Herein lay the core truth and function of Daoism: we must increase our intellect but then shed the layers of our Ego; if we can do this we will attain spiritual transcendence.

Too many of us identify with our emotions and make them who we are. It is important that we recognise that our emotions are a reflection of our Ego, not our true consciousness. The five virtues are the manifestation of true consciousness.

THE FIVE TE (VIRTUES)

According to Daoist thought our true consciousness is the seat of the five virtues. These are five facets of human nature which reflect a pure heart devoid of negativity and imbalance. As these virtues move out of our consciousness into the human mind they must pass through the Ego which distorts them into the five emotions. Through continued Nei Gong practice we are aiming to convert these emotions back into the five virtues which will then shine through and dissolve our false sense of self.

'Follow the ways of Dao and witness the natural birth of Te,

those who don't will be forced to rely on rules to tell them how to act.'

Table 8.2 below shows the five virtues and how they are related to the five emotions.

Table 8.2 **The Wu Xing, Emotions and Virtues**

Element	Emotion	Virtue
Fire	Mania/Joy	Contentment
Earth	Worry	Love/Empathy
Metal	Grief/Sadness	Courage/Conviction
Water	Fear/Paranoia	Clarity
Wood	Anger	Patience

An important distinction can be made between the emotions and the virtues. Human emotions are transient in nature; they are subject to constant change and leave a 'stain' on the Ego. Every emotional disturbance that we experience in life contributes to the formation of more layers of Ego which obscure our true consciousness. The five virtues do not affect us in the same way; they are permanent in nature and not subject to the constant shifts which move us through various cycling emotional states. They are characteristics of human nature born from a place far deeper than our Ego and so do not aid in the formation of our false sense of self.

The virtues may sound a little too 'sage-like' to be real but the truth is that all of us have experienced these virtues throughout our lives at various times. Our true consciousness does shine through in our actions, words and thoughts but unfortunately they are comparatively less frequent than our transient emotions.

CONVERSION OF MANIA/JOY TO CONTENTMENT

Mania/joy and contentment are manifestations of our Fire energy; they are an expression of our Heart energy and the most closely linked of the emotions/virtues to the quality of our Shen.

Like flickering candle flames, feelings of joy/contentment are fleeting. These feelings must be interspaced with periods of negativity and sadness for us to recognise them. If our Fire energy is allowed to burn out of control we will experience a state of mania which greatly disturbs the Shen; when in this state we are literally 'out of our mind'. Thankfully the majority of us only experience states of mania in brief bursts but occasionally this state takes over leading to mental illness.

When our contentment begins to shine through from deep within our true consciousness, it replaces the transient emotions of joy which we have been used to. The 'flickering candle flame' of our Fire energy is converted into a constant, glowing warmth which expands from our core. No longer subject to emotional highs and lows, we are left with a permanent feeling of comfort with ourselves and the outside world which we live in. This is a deeply pleasant state which enables us to see the beauty in our surroundings and the world in general.

CONVERSION OF WORRY TO LOVE/EMPATHY

Worry and love/empathy are manifestations of our Earth energy and are closely linked to our Yi.

Worry is formed mainly from our deluded thoughts which are generated by the Ego. If we are able to end these deluded thoughts and see the world through the eyes of our true consciousness we will begin to convert the energy of worry into love/empathy. When we are able to deal with the people in our lives with love and empathy we are able to attain a level of understanding which was previously beyond our grasp.

Converting worry to love and empathy is the key to unconditional love. This is the pure energy of acceptance which many of us may experience with our own children or parents but not with any other human being. Some may argue that the intimate relationship with their partner is unconditional but is it? Most relationships have conditions placed upon them; they are usually based upon concepts born from the Ego even if people are unaware of this.

When we experience stress throughout our daily lives, this energy is often converted into worry which draws us into ourselves and prevents us from manifesting complete empathy for others. When we are able to break this cycle and allow unconditional love to shine forth from our consciousness we are left with a feeling of deep inner comfort and security.

CONVERSION OF GRIEF/SADNESS TO COURAGE/CONVICTION

Grief/sadness and courage/conviction are manifestations of our Metal energy and closely linked to our corporeal soul (Po) as well as the health of our lungs.

The emotions of Metal energy feel very 'solid'. Like a metallic ore being formed deep within the planet, sadness and grief condense into an almost tangible ball within our centre. This produces a feeling of great discomfort which many of us carry around for the majority of our lives. In extreme cases this can leave us feeling 'shut off' from the rest of the world as our Po is moved into a state of imbalance. Our Po is also linked to the Hun which is the second aspect of what we usually know as our soul. If these two entities are out of balance with each other they can affect our sleep. Dreams are linked to the wanderings of our Hun according to traditional Daoist thought. If the Po is not able to govern the energy of the Hun then these dreams will become stronger resulting in nightmares and disturbed sleep. It is easy to see how dreams of this type can be linked to our feelings of grief and sadness.

When we reach a high enough state in our Nei Gong practice we will find that our grief and sadness are replaced by feelings of courage and conviction. The Metal energy becomes like a finely forged blade which cuts through feelings of grief as well as difficulties we may face in life. Courage and conviction are pure manifestations of our consciousness which are very different from bravado which may cause us to act recklessly. Courage is born from the energy of pure stillness and so does not cause a person to act with unnecessary haste. According to Daoist thought there must be a strong foundation of courage and conviction for a person to maintain their practices and act as a shining beacon for others.

CONVERSION OF FEAR/PARANOIA TO CLARITY

Fear/paranoia and clarity are the Yin and Yang manifestations of Water elemental energy. They are closely related to our Jing and will-power (Zhi).

Fear/paranoia is a constant factor in many people's lives. According to Daoism, fear is created from an inability to see things for what they are. A distorted sense of the nature of reality causes us to think that there is a reason to be afraid and so our Zhi is disturbed. Like water moving through cracks in a rock face, these fears permeate through every aspect of our being until we reach a state of disease.

Clarity is often translated as 'wisdom' but I feel that this term has too many connotations which may lead to misunderstanding. Clarity is not linked to suddenly gaining a great deal more knowledge but rather is an ability to see the nature of reality. There is nothing to fear if we are able to see the world clearly. This is one of the key factors of Daoism.

CONVERSION OF ANGER TO PATIENCE

Anger and patience are manifestations of our Wood elemental energy. They are linked to our ethereal soul (Hun).

Anger is usually born from a lack of patience. It is rare for an incredibly patient person to be subject to sudden outbursts of rage. Although anger is usually a very fleeting emotion it leaves disturbances in the Ego which will in turn make a person more prone to outbursts of anger in the future.

When we are able to balance the emotions and bring forth the virtue of patience we will find that a curious change has taken place within us. Our Hun is linked to our dreams. As we discussed above, the balance of our Hun and our Po dictates how much we dream and how well we sleep at night. If the Hun is allowed to move out of control we will experience vivid dreams which reflect the state of balance between our emotions and inner consciousness. Ancient Daoists as well as contemporary dream analysts looked for patterns within these dreams which could provide life guidance. When our Hun is under control and in a balanced state we no longer dream; this is different from not remembering our dreams when we awake. Instead of the usual dreams that most people are subjected to we will experience a state of inner tranquillity and emptiness which is akin to the states experienced in deep meditation. The only exception to this is when having a dream serves a purpose. Some people have experienced premonitions of the future within their dreams or clarity on something which they had been considering in their life. Daoist theory is divided over whether this is due to the innate knowledge of human consciousness or divine knowledge from some outside source.

STAYING IN THIS STATE

When a person has reached the state of manifesting the five virtues, they have managed to dissolve a great deal of the Ego. It is at this stage that they will find the innate wisdom of enlightenment gradually starting to develop within them. This is not an instant process; rather a person has to stay in this state of balance and continue their personal cultivation whilst the process of spiritual transcendence gradually unfolds within the centre of their Heart-Mind.

It is for this reason that many spiritual traditions prescribed a life of solitude or separation from the rest of the world by joining a monastic community. Here it was considered much easier to cultivate your inner nature without many of the distractions which people are subjected to each day. Daoism is a little different as it does not adhere to the path of monastic life. If you travel in China or Taiwan now you will be able to see Daoist monasteries where monks and nuns practise their meditation away from the outside world. These monasteries were founded a long time after the *Dao De Jing* laid down the original tenets of Daoism and are not part of Laozi's original teachings. It is generally considered more appropriate to live within regular communities where you are able to experience the many facets of life and learn from the effects which they may have upon your Heart-Mind. The majority of the true Daoist practitioners I have met in Asia lived within built-up places like Beijing or Taipei.

The difficulty is staying in the state which you have reached by converting the emotions to virtues whilst your innate wisdom grows. In order to ensure that this takes place you must continue with your daily practice. It is not enough to reach this stage in your development and then stop your training. If you do this it will not be long before the virtues convert back into the emotions and your Ego begins to rebuild its numerous layers around your true consciousness. There are many cases of practitioners reaching a high level of dissolving the Ego only to end their practice thinking that they had reached 'the end'. It is not long before these practitioners return to the state they were in before.

THE INNER LIGHT OF REALISATION

Daoism is a unique spiritual tradition in that it takes the process of inner cultivation and translates it into a tangible process involving various energetic substances. The conversion of your emotions to virtues is no exception. In order for this change to take place we must have a catalyst and that catalyst is our Shen: the highest refinement of internal energy. If we are able to build up a great deal of Shen then it will begin the inner change of our psyche and begin to dissolve the Ego. When this happens we begin to see the 'inner light of realisation'.

'Dao assimilates the false reality into brilliant light,

This is the way of eternal Dao,

so tranquil since before time.'

Remember that the information contained within the vibrational frequency of Shen is translated by the body into a bright white light. When your Shen has reached a sufficient level and begins to dissolve the Ego you will see this light shining brightly before you. At first this light will begin as a small pinpoint but it will quickly expand until it seems as though you are looking at a full moon. This stage of 'staring at the moon' lasts for some time before the light begins to expand further and then fully engulf your vision. It is as though you are bathed in a white light which brings with it a feeling of pure contentment and inner tranquillity which is the experience of the five virtues coming forth.

Practitioners in the past sometimes mistook this light for enlightenment itself. This is not the case. Those seeking an end goal such as this will be disappointed to discover that the light is itself only part of the process and actually not that difficult to attain providing that you train diligently and correctly. The light which you see is not a visualisation or a figment of your imagination. Some contemporary schools of Daoism have translated references of the 'golden light' in classical texts to mean that you have to picture a light shining down on you. This is a misunderstanding which will distract you from the path to Dao. The light which you are aiming to find is so clear and distinct that it leaves you in no doubt of its existence.

It is an interesting phenomenon that during group meditation it is possible to see another person's Shen. During some stages of internal alchemy, the light of your Shen expands around the head and then drops down through the central branch of the thrusting meridian. If a person who has reached this stage walks past you when you are in meditation you may see light moving in front of you and the thrusting meridian can clearly be seen in your mind's eye. It is even possible to see an outline of the person's head with their Shen expanding out in all directions.

We will now discuss the practice of the last two stages in the Nei Gong practice outlined within this book. These are the stages of 'converting the Qi to Shen' and 'converting the Shen to Dao'. Please note that there are some small risks attached to these stages and so you should familiarise yourself with these risks prior to practising the exercises. You should also ensure that you have a solid foundation in the previous stages we have already discussed.

THE CONVERSION OF QI TO SHEN

It is best to carry out the following practice from a sitting position. It is also possible to work with converting the Qi to Shen from a standing position but experience has shown me that students find it much easier when sitting in a meditative posture.

The conversion of Qi to Shen takes place within the middle Dan Tien. The interaction of the energy body and the consciousness which takes place here generates the five elemental energies of the emotions. This means that any direct work we carry out with the middle Dan Tien will also have an effect on our emotional state. It is highly important that we have an awareness of our emotional state before we begin this stage in our Nei Gong practice. If you are experiencing any form of heightened emotion then please do not practise the exercises outlined in this chapter. Focusing on the middle Dan Tien in this manner may cause your emotional state to be magnified; this can be particularly destructive if you are already feeling depressed or angry. Ensure that you are feeling calm and content with your life prior to beginning this practice. For some people this may mean making some life adjustments so that any outside stresses are removed. If you are not able to make these changes for whatever reason then you will have to wait until your life situation is more suitable for middle Dan Tien work.

If you are sure that you are ready to progress then start by practising the Sung breathing technique for a short while. The nature of your Sung breathing will vary depending upon what stage you have reached in this exercise.

Shift your awareness up to the middle Dan Tien area of your body. It is quite common for your awareness to be drawn to the heart rather than the middle Dan Tien when you first start this practice. This is because the physical beating of the heart is very easy for your mind to attach itself to. The sign of your awareness being on the heart rather than your middle Dan Tien is that your heart rate will increase slightly. At this stage in your training you will doubtless have developed a high level of internal awareness and so feeling your heart rate will not be difficult. When you have successfully found the middle Dan Tien you will become aware of the Qi in this area circulating. It will seem as though your chest is slightly spreading open and vibrations can be felt moving within your chest cavity. Successfully attaching your mind to this point will leave you with a feeling of inner comfort provided that you were in the correct mindset prior to beginning the practice.

It is now time to begin adjusting the strength of your focus in order to ensure that you do not disturb the natural function of the middle Dan Tien. Spend some time with your awareness gently hovering over the middle Dan Tien area. To ensure safe progression it is prudent to spend an hour or so on this for the first few times that you begin this practice. The correct level of focus should leave you with the feeling of contentment and internal vibration mentioned above. An incorrect level of focus will begin to change your mood. If you discover that you start to experience waves of emotions moving over you then your awareness is too strong. Do not worry if this happens; it is highly likely that your awareness will be strong in the beginning. The middle Dan Tien is far more delicate than the lower Dan Tien and so the level of focus which you have been using up until now will probably be too strong. It will not take you long to adjust the strength of your awareness accordingly. When you can keep your mind on the middle Dan Tien for roughly an hour without experiencing a shift in your emotions or an increase in heart rate then you are ready to proceed.

Begin to expand your awareness out from the middle Dan Tien into the space around you. Start slowly and take several minutes to bring your awareness out to the surrounding environment as shown in Figure 8.3.

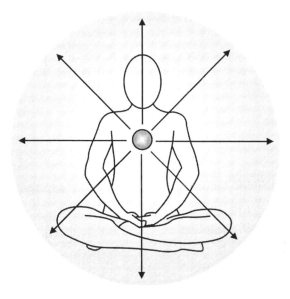

Figure 8.3 Expanding from the Middle Dan Tien

Note that you are not trying to lead Qi from your body or to visualise anything. You are simply expanding your awareness out to the area around you with your middle Dan Tien at the centre. This sphere of mental awareness is enough to act as a catalyst for the conversion of Qi to Shen. The size of your awareness is not important as long as it reaches beyond your body. It can vary from a few feet in every direction to engulfing the entire room you are sitting in. If you have done this correctly you will find that all sense of your body begins to dissolve away as well as any physical feeling of the floor you are sitting on. You will be left with the distinct sensation of being an ethereal entity floating in space. It is at this point that all sense of what is outside and what is inside vanishes. It is difficult to fully describe this experience in writing but you will understand when you experience it for yourself.

The time you are required to remain in this state varies from person to person. Continue practising daily in this manner until your Qi has reached such a level that it begins to convert into Shen. It is now that you will begin to experience the light we discussed earlier in this chapter. At first it will appear as a tiny white dot in front of your vision. It will seem as though somebody has punctured a tiny hole in the darkness allowing a fine beam of white light to shine through. Be patient and with time the white dot will expand until it looks like a full moon sitting in front of you. The 'moon' stage lasts for some time before the light continues to expand.

It is when the bright white light fully engulfs your vision that you will really notice the layers of your Ego beginning to dissolve. Gradually your emotions will begin to convert into the Te and you will naturally begin to change as a person. These changes are not gradual shifts as you might expect; changes in your psyche can be stark and take place quickly. As a word of warning it is worth noting that these changes may be difficult for people who you are close to. The personal development which you are going through will be wholly positive from your point of view but not necessarily in the eyes of your friends and associates. It is an unfortunate fact that most people are slaves to their Ego. They are led by the false sense of self that they have built up around themselves and it is difficult for them to see somebody else escaping from the clutches of their own Ego. Resentment may develop and as with many things in life: change can bring difficulty. It is worth asking yourself whether the changes you are aiming to make to your consciousness are worth the cost.

The white light is not a permanent phenomenon. As with all other parts of the Nei Gong process, the experiences and sensations are only temporary. As your mind grows used to the information contained within the vibrational frequencies of your Jing, Qi and Shen they begin to 'normalise'. The light will stop appearing during your Nei Gong practice although the changes to your psyche will continue. Occasionally you will have a small recurrence of the white light which seems to serve as an indicator that the process is still taking place.

The link between your mind and body are absolute. The other advantage of this stage in your Nei Gong practice is that the changes to your psyche will also underline the changes you have made to your physical body. Your health will have reached an unparalleled level. Your body will be strong and supple with healthy organs and an efficient immune system. There is also one other major effect of the Shen rising to mention: the development of various mental abilities.

SHEN GONG

This is one of the most controversial aspects of Nei Gong. As Shen moves up to the upper Dan Tien it begins to awaken parts of the human consciousness which usually lie dormant within the majority of people. This in turn can give rise to various mental abilities. Many practitioners of the internal arts do not believe in this side of the training and there is a great deal of scepticism with regard to what is possible through your training. I feel that, although controversial, it is important to discuss this area of Nei Gong training which is commonly known as the development of 'Shen Gong'. It is possible to study the internal arts for your entire life and still not come across this side of the training. This may be due to several reasons such as: you have not trained correctly, you have not trained diligently and they are not a part of your system. The last reason can clearly be seen from practitioners of medical Qi Gong. The purpose of medical energy exercises is primarily to improve your health and well-being. They are not designed to convert Qi to Shen and so they will not usually help you to awaken mental abilities of any kind.

It is important to realise that these mental abilities are not a goal in themselves. You should not strive to attain these skills as this is considered a distraction from the true path to Dao. Excessive striving for these abilities will strengthen your Ego and so be detrimental to your progress. I myself have managed to gain some of the skills we will discuss below. At first I was fascinated by what was possible and so they became a large part of what I was teaching. I would use my skills for martial purposes and entertain my class by hurling them around with internal force. After some time I began to become aware of my emotions moving out of control and my health beginning to worsen. I was over-using the mental abilities gained from my practice and they had become the focus of my training. In an effort to correct the damage I had done to myself I ended my teaching for a period of several months which I spent travelling through secluded parts of Asia in an effort to deal with my own mind. This was a very difficult period of time for me which caused a great deal of turmoil within my personal life. Upon my return to the West I began to teach again and used these skills far less; they began to manifest more in my healing practices than in my martial arts. Whereas I would previously use my Shen Gong for combat I now used them to clear blockages from a patient's meridian system and rebalance their energy body. No longer did I notice a detrimental effect on my physical or emotional health and my personal practice has progressed steadily.

'Do not place value on talents and abilities for this will cause competition.

Do not place importance on rare gifts for this will cause the sense to steal.

Do not display anything that will arouse desire for this will disturb the Heart-Mind.'

The first mental ability we should discuss is that of 'empty force'. There has been a great deal of interest in 'empty force' in the martial arts world and a lot of controversy. If you go onto the internet you will find numerous videos of teachers using this skill on their students, some dubious and some real. Empty force is the ability to move or knock down an opponent with no physical contact whatsoever. Qi is projected through empty space from the teacher into his student who usually bounces away from him like a rubber ball, often for quite some distance. Sometimes empty force is combined with a physical touch so that a teacher will lightly touch his students with his fingers and send them flying as though they had been hit by a very powerful force. To an onlooker this can look as if the teacher has supernatural powers and so consequently it is often presumed to be fake. The fact is that empty force is indeed real; it is just misunderstood and often misrepresented by the practitioners of this skill. Some teachers have claimed that empty force is some kind of weapon that can be used to stop any attacker. This is not true. I have met several teachers who used empty force and in each case they could only use the skill on their own students who had trained with them for some time; it was normally useless against a person they had not met before although there are occasional exceptions if a person is particularly sensitive to Qi flow. Does this make empty force fake or useless? No. While it may be useless as a weapon, it is very useful as an internal teaching aid.

Empty force works as Qi and Shen are projected from the practitioner into another person. Remember that Qi and Shen are vibrational waves that carry information. The information contained within this wave is dictated by the mind of the practitioner who has gained the skill of empty force. The information passes into the energy system of the target which then makes the person move around according to the will of their teacher. This relies on the target being energetically awakened enough to interpret the information contained within the Qi being transmitted into them. It does not rely on any form of autosuggestion as the receiver of this information may have their eyes closed and have Qi and Shen projected into their back and yet they still react according to the will of their teacher. A skilled teacher can choose to have their student moved in any direction they want or even in some cases manipulate their body movements to make them squat, run, spin or dance which is often very amusing to watch. The usefulness of this is that the empty force projection moves the target's Qi strongly through their meridians. This induced flow of Qi carries with it information from the teacher's own energy system which helps to awaken the student and move them quickly through the Nei Gong process. In this way empty force is used to pass on the internal teachings of the Daoist arts. While it is true that it may now be used to floor a student, we should reiterate here that it cannot be used to knock down an enemy. There are accounts of this being the case in the past but whether these are true or not I do not know. Perhaps people in the past had reached levels of skill beyond those possible today or maybe the accounts are greatly exaggerated.

It is important that if projecting any form of energy into another person, you have reached a high stage of dissolving your own Ego. A negative mindset or intention will run the risk of damaging the target's energy system. The information from your own Heart-Mind will be passed into the person you are working with and this can lead to them becoming depressed, angry, and manic and may eventually lead to physical illness. A healthy positive feeling of wanting to help your students must be present in order to use empty force safely as a teaching tool. If you have not reached a state of inner contentment then please refrain from using any abilities like this which you may have attained.

Increased intuition is usually the second skill that a person develops. Your mind becomes able to interpret the information contained within a person's aura. You may find that you instinctively know a great deal about people you meet. This information will range from knowledge of their emotional state right through to their current state of health and their medical history. Past traumas in particular sit very heavily within a person's aura and you may suddenly find that you have a flash of information about this past event. Some people find that this information enters their consciousness as a thought whilst others find that they gain visual information. It is very important that this information is used appropriately and that you maintain a strong code of ethics. Most people you come into contact with will not want you to know their deepest secrets. You must never use it to your advantage or let the information give you a feeling of power over other people. If this begins to happen you should immediately take yourself away and continue to work on your own personal development. The Ego must not get involved in the manifestation of these abilities.

A useful skill is an ability to transmit information from yourself into another person for healing purposes. Qi and Shen is transferred in the same way as empty force but the intention is to help a person initiate their own healing process. Healers have used this ability to transfer healing energy from their palms or through tools such as acupuncture needles. If this ability manifests within you then you should be aware of several important factors. First, you need to ensure that you have a high degree of health yourself. Information from your body is passed into your patient; if you are sick, unhealthy or unfit this will have a detrimental effect on the patient's health. Quite simply a healer must be healthy. The second factor to become aware of is that there will be a backlash of information from your patient, particularly from long-term or terminal conditions. Whilst healing your patient may make them feel great, it will begin to take its toll on your own energy system. It is common for energy healers to have their own health crisis at some point in their lives which has been contributed to by their treatments. Some therapists have various mental visualisations which they use to 'shield' themselves from this negative information passing into their own energy systems. I have seen very little evidence of these techniques working very well. Practice of arts like Dao-Yin exercises or Nei Gong is required to purge the negative factors from the energy system. The third major factor to be aware of is, again, your own Ego. It is easy to fall into the trap of feeling very good about yourself when you have 'healed' a patient, especially if they show you a great deal of gratitude. Keep in mind that you did not really heal your patient; you simply enabled their own innate energy system to heal itself. You were only a catalyst for their own natural healing process. Any strengthening of your Ego is detrimental to your own personal progression.

Information on all of the various mental abilities which can be gained from Nei Gong practice could continue for many pages. It is not within the scope of this book to cover this information. It is also only possible to list mental abilities which I have witnessed myself; no doubt there are countless more. During my studies I have witnessed numerous fantastical abilities such as control of the weather, control of a person's emotions, projection of light from the eyes, telepathy, astral projection and many more. Some of these abilities I understand and some I do not.

SHEN GONG IS NOT ENLIGHTENMENT

It is important to note that the various mental abilities mentioned above are gained prior to enlightenment, not after. If you start to develop the ability of empty force or any other psychic skill, it does not mean that you have reached a state of spiritual elevation. Rather, the misuse of these abilities can prevent you from reaching this level.

I have met teachers who used Shen Gong skills to demonstrate to their students that they had achieved enlightenment. Their students looked up to them as though they were some kind of deity and invariably some kind of abuse of power was taking place. I came across one group in Southern Thailand where the teacher was using the ability to control emotions they had gained from esoteric Buddhist practices to control the minds of their followers. Emotions are only informational waves as we have seen. A person with the ability to project Shen can easily control these waves in people around them and it is not sign of being a Buddha. The unscrupulous teacher took a great deal of money from their followers who believed that they were being led towards some kind of salvation. This is not an isolated case and you should be wary of grand claims like this. If you come across a teacher who can manifest these abilities then by all means study with them but keep in mind that they are only normal people who are subject to the same flaws of character as everybody else.

Box 8.1 Combining Nei Gong with Nei Jia

Nei Jia is the collective name for the internal martial arts. The three most commonly practised Nei Jia are Taiji, Xingyiquan and Baguazhang although there are also less common Nei Jia such as Taihequan, Taiyiquan, Yiquan and Liuhebafa. The Japanese art of Aikido also has a great many internal elements incorporated into its training.

Nei Gong is an excellent adjunct to any form of Nei Jia training. The various stages of development in the internal martial arts directly reflect the stages of progression in Nei Gong. Once the body has been correctly relaxed, opened and aligned when moving and when stationary it is time to begin awakening the various elements of the energy body. Practising Nei Gong alongside your regular martial training will speed up this process.

'The highest warrior aims to end all fighting,

The skilled warrior fights without anger.

They defeat their opponent without engaging them,

This is the Te of non-contending.'

The main difference between pure Nei Gong training and Nei Jia training is that you practise partner work and your movements generally have a martial intent behind them. In this instance you should be aware of one important factor: your Yi. Your Yi or intention dictates the quality of the information contained within the Qi which is transmitted to your partner during a sparring drill or strike. To put it simply, a positive feeling of warmth and compassion will have a positive effect on their energy body whilst a negative intention full of hate and a desire to dominate will be bad for them. Even a light strike combined with an awakened energy system and a negative intention has the potential to cause damage. This was one of the reasons for teachers in the temples of old teaching their students philosophy and ethics. Who would want to train an efficient fighter with no ethics or regard for human life? If you combine Nei Gong with Nei Jia it is imperative that you spend a great deal of time 'soul searching' and working on your inner nature.

Internal force with a positive intention is best practised from a set platform like pushing hands (Tui Shou) which any Taiji practitioner should be familiar with. Once your energy system is fully awakened and Qi is flowing effectively your partner will be lifted high into the air and thrown away from you without it causing them any harm. Your partner is often confused to find that they begin to laugh uncontrollably for some time after they land on the floor in front of you. If you can attain this skill then you are on the road to understanding the meaning of the Nei Jia.

RETURNING TO EMPTINESS: CONVERTING SHEN TO DAO

The highest stage of development in your Nei Gong practice is converting your accumulated Shen back into emptiness. There is a great deal of material written about this stage in Daoist and Buddhist classical texts although they use different language to explain the same process. Much of this information is presented in metaphorical language which is difficult to understand, particularly within Daoist writings. Once you are able to understand the hidden teachings within these texts, the process becomes quite clear. This section will discuss the practice of converting your Shen to Dao from a Daoist perspective and so use their language rather than Buddhist terminology although I would recommend that those who want to read further into this area of Nei Gong practice also consult Buddhist texts.

It is important to see that there are two main divisions of practice within Daoism. The original teachings and methods of Laozi were concerned with converting Shen into Dao which would allow a person to attain true emptiness. Later in the development of Daoism it was taught that a person should develop what is commonly known as a 'spiritual embryo' which would continue to live after the practitioner's death. This was the key to attaining spiritual immortality. This 'spiritual embryo' was nurtured in the practitioner's energy body for several years before it was allowed to leave the body through the crown and travel freely during meditation practice. Tales of this practice mirror reports of astral projection which is a phenomenon which has been reported in both the Eastern and the Western worlds. The theory is that the embryo travels up to the enlightened realm upon the practitioner's death where it escapes the cycle of rebirth and continues to live as a holy being. Some Daoist practices aim to communicate with these divine beings in the hope of gaining spiritual guidance. In a way these spiritual immortals are seen in the same way as guardian angels are in the West.

The original teachings of Laozi do not mention the nurturing or development of the 'spiritual embryo'. This was an idea developed much later when the alchemists of the Daoist sects began their search for eternal life. Laozi instead spoke of attaining true emptiness and opening the 'mysterious pass' which we mentioned briefly in Chapter 2.

Many practitioners have sought the location of the mysterious pass within their body. The location of the mysterious pass has been sought within the three Dan Tien, the centre of the brain and countless other locations around the energy system. This is as logical as ingesting external substances in order to gain immortality (a practice which killed many alchemists). The mysterious pass is 'located' within the centre of the three main bodies of man when they move into complete harmony. Figure 8.4 shows the location of the mysterious pass.

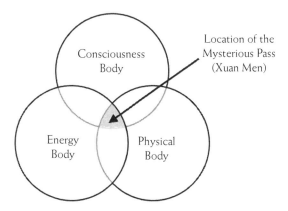

Figure 8.4 Location of the Mysterious Pass

The three bodies have been moving into complete balance throughout your Nei Gong training. By the time you reach this stage you should have fully awakened the energy system which is now functioning as a single entity with your physical body. Your consciousness has been moving into balance through the conversion of Qi to Shen and the dissolving of the Ego. The bright white light of your Shen should have flooded to entirely fill your vision and now passed so as to return you to darkness. It is only at this point that the mysterious pass begins to open and the origin of existence can be comprehended by the practitioner.

> *'The sage embraces the union of the three realms*
>
> *and thus becomes the master under Heaven.*
>
> *The Sage discards the false sense of self.*
>
> *He therefore finds the white light of cultivation.'*

Note that I am a practitioner of both Nei Gong and Daoist meditation. I have spent many years reaching the stage I am now studying at but

I am not an enlightened being. The opening of the mysterious pass is a long stage which can take an entire lifetime. It is said that it is also possible to open the mysterious pass in an instant; I have not been so fortunate. I have had glimpses of the opening of the mysterious pass but not been able to sustain this state for protracted lengths of time. I will discuss the theory of locating and opening the mysterious pass along with the experiences which accompany this stage but I cannot lead you past this point. Once you manage to work through the Nei Gong practices in this book, you will have to seek out a qualified master (if you have not already) who can guide you deeper into Daoist meditation.

When the mysterious pass opens you will experience the meaning of complete emptiness which is also known as 'stillness'. It is now that you will experience what the Daoists call 'foetal breathing'. Foetal breathing is when the physical process of respiration ends and your energy system takes over. Some Daoist texts refer to it as becoming like a 'dead man' which is an accurate description indeed. The first time your lungs stop working can be very disconcerting indeed. The first time I experienced this was during a very deep meditation. My mind had totally stilled and I had sunk into the state of emptiness which I had been striving for in my practice for so long. It was then that my mind realised that I was no longer breathing. The stillness of my mind was shattered by the sudden feeling of being suffocated and I felt as though I was drowning. I gasped for air very loudly and grabbed my chest which disturbed the group I was meditating with. It took me some time to get back to this stage and even longer to keep my mind still and undisturbed by this strange phenomenon.

As well as your lungs ceasing to function, your heart stops beating and your blood is said to stop flowing around your body. Obviously this completely contradicts what we would say is possible in Western science but it has been confirmed not just by myself but by countless practitioners of meditation throughout history. This is the meaning of true emptiness.

'He who can still his consciousness and end his breathing,

Will be sure to attain immortality.'

When the physical act of breathing ceases, the energy body takes over and begins to 'breathe' in harmony with the pulsing energies of

Heaven and Earth. It is said that if you are able to maintain this stage of foetal breathing for a protracted length of time, the mysterious pass will fully open and the nature of existence will be yours to behold. I cannot confirm this but I can discuss two other interesting occurrences which are a sign of the early stages of this process: the opening of the 'tunnel' and the attainment of 'Wu Wei'.

When the 'foetal breathing' takes over you will become aware of your energy system expanding and contracting far beyond the limits of your body. All sense of your physical form is gone and the concept of space is no more. You will doubtless have already experienced the stage of your mind expanding out in all directions when your Shen had reached a high stage. This is the stage of feeling as though you were an ethereal entity suspended in space discussed earlier in this chapter. The feeling of losing any concept of space is very different. You will still be unaware of your physical form but now you are not sure whether or not you have expanded out in all directions or whether the space around you has contracted in on you.

Your experience of this stage will vary with each sitting session. Sometimes it seems as though your mind has completely filled the macrocosm whilst at other times it seems as though the macrocosm has shrunk to a few inches across and your consciousness is trapped within it. At first this feeling is not altogether comfortable and can feel a little claustrophobic but once your mind has become used to it you will feel very at home in this state.

It is now that the 'tunnel' opens. In the same location where the white light of your Shen first appeared a hazy white tunnel of light appears. It stretches away in front of you and rotates slowly. It seems as though the tunnel of light is connected to your forehead in the location which many cultures know as the 'third eye'. When you see the white tunnel, it is easy to understand why the mysterious pass got its name. The balancing of the three bodies of man produces a vision which seems as though a spiritual gateway has been opening in front of you. It is not lost on me that this experience is very similar to accounts given by people who have died on operating tables and had 'out of body' experiences. It is common for people who have had near-death experiences to talk of seeing the white tunnel which they feel compelled to travel along. It is not my experience that you begin to travel down this tunnel during meditation practice; it remains extended out in front of you and rotates slowly whilst your energy body continues to breathe for you and your mind rests in stillness.

This stage is a very comforting stage. In your mind you feel completely at ease and it is with some disappointment that your practice ends and you have to return to the outside world. It is easy for me to understand why practitioners in the past who have reached this stage disappeared into the mountains and became hermits. Their practice gave them such a feeling of spiritual comfort that they wished to have more time to focus on their training. There is a personal struggle to be had here. By this time you will already have drawn the benefits of emotional stillness, excellent health, inner wisdom and more. Perhaps this is enough for you? To go further at this time would mean to leave the physical world and retreat into your inner universe. No doubt you will be as tempted as I when you reach this stage but what of the people around you and the responsibilities in your life? Is it fair to leave that all behind and satisfy your own desire for spiritual elevation? According to Daoist thought it is not. Traditionally there was a period of intense training which was followed by a long period of teaching and passing on your knowledge to benefit others. Some Daoists taught various martial arts to benefit people's physical health whilst others practised medicine in their local communities. Compassion was known as one of the treasures of Daoism. It was considered far more important that personal attainment. Perhaps if you manage to reach this stage it is wise to wait for the desired solitude until you have reached much later in life. If you practise well then you will maintain your health and vigour into old age anyway so you will not be short of time. In my mind the great compassion and wisdom to be gained from the practice of internal arts such as Nei Gong is wasted if it is not shared with others. This was always the Daoist ideal: to spread goodness throughout the world and effect change upon society.

'Persist in emptying your Heart-Mind,

Thus you will attain the purity of Wu Wei.

Act without accruing to attain union with Dao.'

No discussion of Daoist ideals would be complete without discussing the term 'Wu Wei'. This term is widely used within contemporary Daoist teachings. The term is usually translated as meaning 'without doing'. This spreads the view that Daoists are lazy people who never work very hard during the course of their lives. This is simply not true. A lazy, complacent Daoist has completely missed the point. The character 'Wei' can also be translated as meaning 'to govern' which means Wu Wei could mean 'to act without governing'. This is a far better translation for the term Wu Wei. To act 'without governing' is the Daoist concept of cause and effect. According to Heart-Mind theory it is impossible to generate a thought, action or word without engaging the Ego. This distorts the information being transmitted to and from the person which in turn builds further layers of the false sense of self which surrounds our true consciousness. This vicious cycle of cause and effect is constantly moving us further from enlightenment as we have already discussed at the start of this chapter. This is the same as the Buddhist view of Karma. To act within the principle of Wu Wei is to think, speak and act without the Ego governing us. This is considered to be acting in accord with the will of Heaven which also acts without governing. Within Chinese thought, true human consciousness is given to us at birth by Heaven itself.

When your internal development has reached a high stage you will begin to experience acting according to the principle of Wu Wei in your everyday life. An internal awareness will develop of the effect your speech, thoughts and actions have upon the outside world and the people you interact with. It is as though you suddenly become aware of the multi-faceted web of cause and effect which entangles all sentient beings. Like viewing a fragile balance of human emotions you become intuitively aware of how one simple word generated by the Ego can have a knock-on effect which is steadily amplified like a snowball rolling down a hill. More importantly you become aware of how your words, actions and thoughts no longer have such an effect upon this fragile balance. I sat with a monk in the mountains of China who explained the concept of Wu Wei to me by throwing pebbles into some water. Each pebble created several concentric ripples which spread across the surface of the water. He then threw a handful of pebbles into the water which generated hundreds of ripples which spread out and mixed in with each other. The surface of the water was in turmoil. He then stated that acting according to Wu Wei was like being able to throw a pebble into the water without generating any ripples; laughing, he apologised that he would not be able to demonstrate that.

The stage of becoming aware of cause and effect begins to develop a strong sense of presence in everything that you do. You become acutely aware of the damaging effect of the Ego and realise how all of the evils of the world are caused by the false sense of self which grips on to most people. Gradually this will begin to change how you interact with people and gradually your words, actions and thoughts begin to have a very positive effect on people. Like medicine for the consciousness, Wu Wei begins to spread through the people around you who find that their Egos begin to dissolve through interacting with you. This is the stage of acting as a sage: a subtle teacher who remains hidden behind the scenes. This is the stage of 'acting without governing' but still effecting positive change in the world.

This is quite simply the most important aspect of Daoism. All of your practices amount to little if you do not practise the compassionate principle of Wu Wei. As Laozi stated:

'The sage does not attain things for himself,

He helps others and so in return he gains much,

Heaven's way is to give and not do harm,

The sage's way is to act in accord with Heaven.'

CONCLUSION

Nei Gong is still a relatively unknown aspect of the internal arts. Over the last few years writers have begun using the term Nei Gong more frequently and now there are several teachers passing this information on in the Western world. Still some people who have read this book may be asking where they can gain instruction in the practice of Nei Gong. The answer is simple: you can find it anywhere. Remember that Nei Gong is not a system in its own right; it is a process of internal change. Anybody who studies more widespread arts such as Qi Gong or Taiji can begin to study Nei Gong providing the fundamental principles that are being passed on to them by their teacher are correct. Nei Gong is a mindset. If you are still focused largely on the techniques and collecting external body movements then you will never progress past the surface levels of your training. If you engage your mind and explore the possibilities, train hard and study the classical texts of Daoism diligently your existing practices will be more than adequate to lead you into the deeper aspects of the Daoist arts. While it is true that a qualified master can guide you in the correct direction, they do not hold any magical keys which cannot be gained through consistent training and sincere study. The Daoist belief of already holding the wisdom within the centre of your true consciousness can readily be experienced through dedicated training. Start at the beginning; condition your physical body, spend a realistic amount of time on this stage and then only when the time is right should you begin to progress on to awakening the energy body. The vast majority of long-term Qi Gong and Taiji practitioners should already have had some experiences around this stage on internal development and indeed maybe some aspects of this book have 'rung bells' when you were reading it. Perhaps you could identify with some experience which you have not previously been able to understand or explain. If this is the case then you should be able to see which aspects of Nei Gong you are already practising without realising and then strengthen this process through the development of a steady internal awareness.

Daoism is an esoteric art which is born from Chinese culture. Sometimes this can seem like a very alien culture which defies any form of logic. We have a tendency in the West to try and explain everything from a purely scientific standpoint when in fact science can only explain so many things. When practising the internal arts it is vitally important to keep this in mind. Whilst it is healthy to acknowledge the scientific basis for some aspects of Nei Gong training it is equally important to understand that much of it cannot be explained in a conventional Western scientific way. Western science is relatively young whilst Daoism is based upon several thousand years of accumulated experiential learning. Question everything you do, carefully consider everything you are taught but remember to do so with an open mind and an open heart. This is the way to get in touch with your true consciousness and the universal truth contained within.

Over the last few years I have been teaching the internal arts in the UK and passing on the exact method which I myself train in. Many of my students have delved deep into the various stages of Nei Gong training which are contained within this book. I have witnessed them going through great processes of internal change. I have seen improvements in their physical health and well-being. I have witnessed emotional difficulties slowly fade away and taken great pleasure in watching the dawning of realisation spread across my students' faces like a beaming smile.

Throughout this book I have tried to make it clear that the highest stages of Nei Gong development can only be attained through protracted dedicated study and indeed many practitioners who come across this aspect of the internal arts are compelled to devote a great deal of their time to their personal training. That being said, many of the physical and psychological health benefits which can be drawn from the early stages of Nei Gong training can be experienced even by those who only train a little. The bottom line is that the Dao is accessible by everyone in one way or another. The form it takes only depends upon how much you are willing to put in.

In conclusion I would like to end with some of the most profound words of Laozi which are from the very first section of the *Dao De Jing*:

> *'He who can free his mind eternally of desire and attachment*
>
> *will perceive the very essence of Dao.*
>
> *He who is not free of desire and attachment*
>
> *will only encounter the outer forms of this world.'*

This is truly the key to effective Nei Gong and spiritual liberation.

APPENDIX

The diagram on the following page shows the formation of acquired Qi from the food we eat and the air we breathe into our lungs. It also shows the movement of Qi through the body according to the various functions of the organs and the rotation of the lower Dan Tien.

Please note that this is only a very simplified diagram and the inter-relationships of the organs are complex. There are far more relationships than are shown on this diagram but it should be sufficient for readers to grasp the main movements of Qi through the body.

For more detailed information please refer to any comprehensive Chinese medicine textbook.

Note that some of the functions of the organs according to Chinese medicine theory differ greatly from the Western understanding.

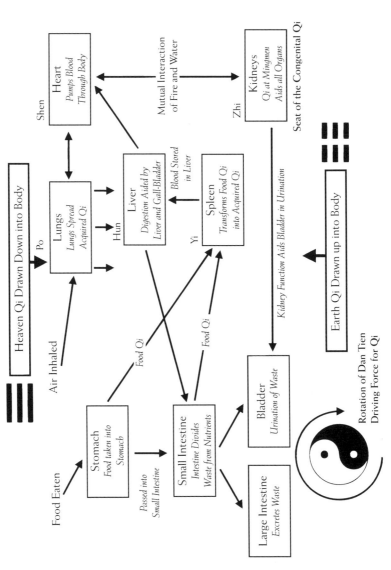

Figure A.1 Formation and Movement of Qi in the Body

Glossary of Pinyin Terms

The following glossary of pinyin terms contains Chinese terminology used throughout this book. Simplified Chinese characters have been included for reference purposes apart from where traditional Chinese characters are still commonly used as in the case of Chinese medical terminology.

Baihui 百會 (GV20) An acupuncture point situated on top of the head. Translated as meaning 'hundred meetings' due to it being the meeting place for the six Yang meridians. In classical Daoism it is also the point where numerous spirits converge.

Da Zhou Tian 大周天 'Large heavenly cycle', also known as the large water wheel of Qi. This is the primary circulation of energy out of the body which can be achieved through consistent alchemy or Nei Gong training.

Dan Tien 丹田 Usually refers to the lowest of the three main 'elixir fields'. Its primary function is the conversion of Jing to Qi and moving the Qi throughout the meridian system.

Dao 道 The nameless and formless origin of the universe. Daoism is the study of this obscure concept and all internal arts are a way of experientially understanding the nature of Dao.

Dao De Jing 德道经 Can be translated as 'The virtue of following the way'. The classical text of Daoism written by the great sage Laozi. Also written as *Dao De Jing*.

Dui 兑 One of the eight trigrams of Daoist Bagua theory. Its energetic manifestation is metaphorically likened to a lake although Dui does not directly mean lake.

Feng Shui 风水 'Wind and water'. This is the Daoist study of environmental energies and the influence of the macrocosm upon the human energy system and consciousness.

Gen 艮 One of the eight trigrams of Daoist Bagua theory. Its energetic manifestation is likened to that of a mountain.

Gua 卦 'Trigram'. These are the eight sacred symbols which make up Daoist Bagua theory. They are a way to conceptualise the various vibrational frequencies of the energetic realm and how they interact.

Huiyin 會陰 (CV1) 'Meeting of Yin' is an acupuncture point located at the perineum. It is named after the fact that it is situated within the most Yin area of the human body.

Hun 魂 'Yang soul' is the ethereal soul which continues to exist after our death. It is usually housed within the liver.

Ji Ben Qi Gong 基本气功 'Fundamental energy exercises': the eight basic level exercises outlined within this book. The primary exercises taught within the Lotus Nei Gong School of internal arts which is based in the UK.

Jing 精 The lowest vibrational frequency of the three main energetic substances of man. Usually translated as meaning 'essence' and often misunderstood as being human sexual fluids.

Jing Gong 精功 'Essence exercises': the technique of building up and refining our Jing.

Jing Luo 经络 The human meridian system which is made up of numerous energetic pathways which regulate the body and transport Qi to and from our organs and tissues.

Kan 坎 One of the eight trigrams of Daoist Bagua theory which is usually likened to the energetic manifestation of water.

Kun 坤 One of the eight trigrams of Daoist Bagua theory. Its energetic manifestation is usually likened to that of the planet.

Laogong 劳宫 (PC8) An acupuncture point situated in the centre of the palm. Its name means 'palace of toil' due to it being on the human hand which carries out a lot of physical work. Within Daoism they also know this point to be very important in venting heat from the heart and so it is rarely at rest. It is a very important point in Qi Gong practice as it regulates the internal temperature and also allows us to emit Qi in practices such as external Qi therapy.

Laozi 老子 The great sage. The original Daoist who wrote the *Dao De Jing*. Supposedly left this text with a border watchmen when he retreated into hermitage in the western mountains of China.

Li 離 One of the eight trigrams of Daoist Bagua theory. Its energetic manifestation is usually likened to fire.

Ming 命 Your predestined journey from life to death. Usually translated as meaning 'fate' but this really does not explain the true meaning of the term.

Mingmen 命門 (GV4) An acupuncture point in the lower back which is very important in Nei Gong practice. This point is referred to several times in this book and serious internal arts practitioners should work very hard to awaken the energy in this area of their meridian system.

Nei Gong 內功 The process of internal change and development which a person may go through if they practise the internal arts to a high level.

Po 魄 The 'Yin soul' which dies with the human body. Largely connected to our physical sense, the Po resides in the lungs.

Qi 氣 'Energy'. A term that is often difficult to translate into English. In Nei Gong theory it is an energetic vibration which transports information through the energy system.

Qi Gong 氣功 Usually gentle exercises which combine rhythmic movements with breathing exercises to shift Qi through the body. The term means 'energy exercises' although it is sometimes translated as meaning 'breathing exercises'.

Qi Hai 氣海 (CV6) An acupuncture point which sits in front of the lower Dan Tien. Its name in English means 'sea of Qi' as it is the point from where Qi is generated and where it flows from. Like water returning to the sea in rivers and streams, Qi returns to the lower Dan Tien when it circulates in the 'small water wheel of Qi'.

Qian 乾 One of the eight trigrams of Daoist Bagua theory. Its energetic manifestation is usually likened to the movements of Heaven.

Ren 人 Within Daoism, Ren is 'humanity'. Humanity sits between Heaven and Earth and is a reflection of their fluctuations and movements. Ren is nourished by Earth and stimulated to development through Heaven.

Shen 神 The energy of consciousness. Vibrates at a frequency close to that of Heaven. It is manifested within the body as a bright white light.

Shen Gong 神功 This is the arcane skill of working with the substance of consciousness. Within Daoism it is said that a skilled Shen Gong practitioner can manipulate the very energy of the environment.

Sun 巽 One of the eight trigrams of Daoist Bagua theory. Its energetic manifestation is usually likened to that of the wind.

Sung 松 This is the process of transferring habitual tension from the physical or consciousness body into the energetic realm where it can be dissolved.

Taiji 太极 A Daoist concept of creation which can be translated as meaning the 'motive force of creation'.

Te 德 The congenital manifestation of the transient emotions. Te is born from deep within the true human consciousness which is usually buried beneath the various layers of the Ego.

Tian 天 'Heaven'. Not to be mistaken for the Christian concept of Heaven, this refers to the vibrational frequency of the macrocosm. Within the microcosm of the body Heaven is used metaphorically to refer to human consciousness.

Tui Na 推拿 A form of Chinese medical massage which means 'push and grab'.

Wu Xing 五行 The five elemental energies which are an important part of Daoist creation theory, psychology and medicine.

Wuji 无极 The Daoist concept of non-existence. The blank canvas upon which reality is projected and an important part of Daoist creation philosophy.

Xin-Yi 心意 'Heart-Mind'. This is the framework with which we attempt to understand the various aspects of human consciousness. Originally a Buddhist concept, it was absorbed into Daoist teachings.

Yang Qi 阳氣 Our internal Qi which moves out toward the surface of the body and the congenital meridians.

Yang Shen Fa 养身法 Literally 'life-nourishing principles'. This is the Daoist practice of living healthily which should be studied alongside all internal arts.

Yi 意 'Intention' or 'awareness'. An important element of human consciousness to cultivate in Nei Gong training.

Yi Jing 易经 The *Classic of Change*. An ancient Daoist text which is based upon Bagua theory.

Yin Qi 阴 Our internal Qi which moves in to nourish the organs of the body.

Yongquan 涌泉 (K1) An acupuncture point on the base of the foot which means 'bubbling spring'. This is the main point through which Earth Energy is drawn into the body.

Zang Fu 脏腑 The collective name for the Yin and Yang organs of the body.

Zhen 震 One of the eight trigrams of Daoist Bagua theory. Its energetic manifestation is often likened to thunder.

Zhi 志 An element of human consciousness which is directly linked to the state of our kidneys. The nearest translation in English is 'will-power'.

Ziran 自然 The Daoist philosophical concept of acting in harmony with nature and returning to an original state.

BIBLIOGRAPHY

Buell, P. and Ramey, D. (2004) 'A true history of acupuncture.' *Focus on Alternative and Complementary Therapies 9*, 269–273.

Cleary, T. (1986) *The Daoist I Ching*. Boston, MA: Shambhala Publications Inc.

Cleary, T. (1996) *Opening the Dragon Gate*. Boston, MA: Tuttle Publishing.

Maciocia, G. (1989) *The Foundations of Chinese Medicine*. Edinburgh: Churchill Livingstone.

Maoshing, N. (1995) *The Yellow Emperor's Classic of Medicine*. Boston, MA: Shambhala Publishing inc.

Reid, D. (1993) *Guarding the Three Treasures*. Sydney: Simon and Schuster.

Reid, D. (1998) *A Complete Guide to Chi Gung*. Boston, MA: Shambhala Publications Inc.

Waley, A. (1999) *Laozi*. Hunan: Hunan People's Publishing House.

ABOUT THE AUTHOR

Damo Mitchell was born into a family of martial artists and so began his training at the age of four. This training has continued throughout his life and expanded to include the study of both internal and external martial arts, meditation and various aspects of Chinese medicine as well as Nei Gong. His studies have taken him across the planet in search of authentic masters of the spiritual traditions and he spends his time studying, travelling and teaching.

Damo is the technical director of the Lotus Nei Gong School of Daoist Arts which is based in the UK although Damo also teaches in other parts of Europe. More information can be found on the main website of his school: www.lotusneigong.com.

INDEX